Are You A Narcissist?

The Ultimate Guide to Finding Out If You Suffer From Narcissism and the Narcissistic Personality Disorder

By Larry Tate

I0435870

Table of Contents

Introduction...5

Chapter 1: Why it matters if you are becoming a narcissist...10

Chapter 2: How to identify whether or not you are a narcissist.. 22

Chapter 3: Do you suffer from Narcissistic Personality Disorder?...35

Chapter 4: How narcissism impacts your ability to relate to others 46

Chapter 5: The powerful force of narcissism in the workplace..65

Chapter 6: When you can't see the world as others see it...79

Chapter 7: When life means never having to say you're sorry 98

Chapter 8: How narcissists can take bragging to a new dimension...107

Chapter 9: The darkest side of narcissism 115

Chapter 10: How narcissists use others to achieve their own ends 121

Chapter 11: Why we all need a healthy dose of narcissism 131

Chapter 12: The broader scope of narcissism.. 154

Conclusion 169

Introduction

In our fast-paced, impersonal world, we all need to love ourselves a little.

We need to find some worth within us, to believe that we are capable of loving and being loved. We need to know we have a reasonable chance of achieving our goals and making our way through the maze of life's challenges.

But what happens when our view of ourselves becomes totally distorted from reality? What happens when we falsify who we are and create an image that, while grand and important, has no root in reality?

We may be treading on the quicksand of narcissism, a mental disorder.

We fall off the edge of a healthy self-confidence and into a world of exaggerated self-importance. The line between our fantasy world and our real world blurs.

Unchecked, we can progress to Narcissistic Personality Disorder where we admire ourselves so much we can summon only contempt for others. Our whole world becomes compromised. We cannot build and enjoy lasting relationships, our work life is endangered and we become angry and stressed at a world that just doesn't measure up to our high demands. In some cases, suicidal thoughts can occur.

Narcissism and Narcissistic Personality Disorder should concern everyone, especially for those who experience the symptoms and those who view them in others. That is because it is a growing problem in developing countries throughout the world, particularly in youthful populations.

Unlike any previous time in history, we are seeing increased numbers of people experiencing symptoms of Narcissistic Personality Disorder and the unhappiness that accompanies it.

The trend first appeared on the horizon in 2008 when researchers at the National Institutes of Health discovered that almost 10 per cent of Americans in their 20s had experienced some form of the disorder in their lives.

The study, published in the *Journal of Clinical Psychiatry,* supported other research conducted at American universities. Another study, that included 35,000 Americans of all ages, indicated that one out of every 16 people had experienced what they described as clinical Narcissistic Personality Disorder during their lives.

If you find yourself exaggerating your achievements when you discuss yourself with friends and new acquaintances, if you day-dream constantly about being honored for your power, brilliance or beauty, if you honestly believe that you are superior to everyone around you, and if you don't mind taking advantage of other people to get what you want, you are already exhibiting narcissistic tendencies.

If you are envious of other people and require constant attention and admiration, you are also in danger of letting narcissism lead you down a dark road in life.

The good news is that if caught early, narcissistic tendencies can be stemmed. You can bring yourself back from the brink with home remedies and a designated plan of action.

In advanced cases, clinical therapy is effective.

Narcissism is not a personality disorder that needs to be treated with medications or massive change. Rather, for most people, a conscious plan for small changes can restore balance in your personality. Talk therapy programs with trained professionals also have yielded good results.

This book explores the whole idea of how much we love ourselves and when we cross over into the land of too much.

We have combed all the recent scientific studies published in peer-reviewed journals and brought them together in straightforward terms so you fully comprehend all the aspects of narcissism and Narcissistic Personality Disorder.

In the coming chapters we will show you how to:

- Determine if you are exhibiting the signs of narcissism and Narcissistic Personality Disorder
- Illustrate the impact of an exaggerated sense of self-worth on your ability to relate to others
- Study the difficulties of being or working with a narcissist in the workplace
- Help you to see the world from the perspective of other people
- Delve into the narcissist's inability to apologize
- Examine why we pretend to be more important than we are
- Explore the darkest sides of narcissism such as rage and contempt at everyone around you
- Calculate the true cost of using other people to advance your own agenda

We will also discuss why we all need a certain amount of narcissism to lead healthy lives.

Finally, we will look at the reasons why narcissism as a personality disorder is on the rise in our current culture and the factors that are fueling its growth.

Whether you are living with someone who suffers from narcissism or whether you recognize yourself as someone sliding in that direction, this book is an intriguing read into a personality disorder that was identified generations ago, but is more prevalent in our modern world than ever before.

Chapter 1: Why it matters if you are becoming a narcissist

To experience true, mature and fulfilling love, you must first love yourself.

But what if you love yourself too much?

What if you become totally obsessed with yourself to the point that you start to block out other people from your life? What if you become a narcissist or develop Narcissistic Personality Disorder?

To the world, you may appear beautiful, charming and sophisticated. You may even appear kind.

But as people get closer to you, they discover to their horror that what initially looks attractive is just a mirage. Your outward image is just a shallow two-dimension picture and the other dimension, the real you, is very unattractive and self-centered indeed.

You are a master manipulator and a fake. You use anyone who gets close to you to achieve your own ends, no matter the cost to them.

When people really get to know you, they dislike you intensely. Those who are really kind might feel sorry for you for being so wrapped up in yourself, but most will just avoid you.

But that doesn't really matter, because for a while at least, your own love is all you want and need to sustain yourself.

But over time, your inner world begins to take over your outer world. It gets more difficult to disengage yourself from your fantasies of power, beauty and tremendous accomplishment with your real world in which you are alarmingly average.

One day you wake up and the movie you are directing of your life has no script. You start to feel depressed. You cannot secure sufficient admiration to fuel your days. The downward spiral starts and before long, you are having suicidal thoughts.

Without effective therapy, there is no "happily ever after" to the all-encompassing love story you have with yourself.

Although narcissism and Narcissistic Personality Disorder are more in the spotlight these days because of a flurry of tests showing the self-esteem of young people is on the rise, it has long been identified as the root of a mental and behavioral disorder.

The word narcissism itself comes from Narcissus, a mythical but very handsome Greek man whose story was popularized by the Roman poet Ovid in his work *The Metamorphoses* (Book of Transformations) written in 8 AD.

Narcissus, a hunter from Thespiae, was an exceptionally proud man who had nothing but disdain from the people around him.

As the story goes, he was walking in the woodland one day when Echo, a mountain nymph, chanced upon him and fell in love with him at first sight. She followed him and when he kept calling out "Who's there?" she finally stepped from the forest shadows and tried to embrace him.

Narcissus roughly rejected her. She was then so heartbroken that she wandered her life away alone in the woodland until only an echo of her remained.

The Goddess of Revenge in Greek mythology, Nemesis, was angry about Narcissus's treatment of Echo. She decided to settle the score.

Nemesis lured Narcissus to a calm pool of water where he could clearly see his own reflection. Being extremely handsome but apparently not too smart, Narcissus didn't realize all he was seeing was a reflection. He fell madly and totally in love with the reflection of himself.

After a period of time, he finally figured out that his love for himself was unrequited. Sadly, he ended up committing suicide.

If you don't like that ending, some later versions of the story have him ultimately changing into a flower that is to this day named after him, the narcissus.

Despite some fictional works dealing with narcissism, it wasn't until 1911 when the first academic study specifically focused on narcissism was published.

Author Otto Rank, an Austrian psychoanalyst and a close friend and colleague of Sigmund Freud for 20 years before the two had a philosophical falling out, linked narcissism to vanity and self-admiration.

Three years later, Sigmund Freud produced a paper called *On Narcissism: An Introduction*.

Even now, Freud's work is interesting because it suggests that obsessive self-love is not as abnormal as people originally thought. To Freud, a degree of narcissism was an ordinary part of the human psyche. Without it, he suggested, we might lose our drive for self-preservation. Good narcissism, such as ordinary self-love, was something he called "primary" narcissism.

Freud figured we all need some kind of ego to get by in this world. It is, in innocent terms, the better self towards which we all strive.

If you have ever wished for something and considered it might be possible to attain it, or if you have summoned your will power to do something a bit extraordinary, you are practicing "primary" narcissism.

In "secondary" narcissism, more of a megalomania develops and this can lead to more serious psychological disorders.

Freud's therapeutic suggestion for treating narcissism was to encourage the narcissist to give away some of their self-love to another person. When they see that the well of love fills up again by the love that is returned to them, they will become more balanced.

Today, psychologists still consider narcissism a difficult condition to treat because since true narcissists believe they are perfect and that the problems lie with everyone else, it is hard to convince them they need treatment. By the time a major crisis like a suicide attempt brings them into therapy, the problem has reached a seriously advanced state.

Nonetheless, modern science shows, as we will outline in upcoming chapters of this book, that there are legitimate treatments for narcissism today that involve a range of different therapies. In the early stages, when it is still possible to recognize yourself in the symptoms, there are actually small behavioral changes you can make on your own to curb it.

If you have Narcissistic Personality Disorder, besides going through life with a highly inflated sense of your own value, you also desperately require endless admiration. You have no feelings of empathy for other people and yet, despite your disdain for them, even the slightest bit of criticism you receive from them can send you into a full tailspin.

The more attention you need and the more accomplished you need to feel, the harder it will be on you if the world does not continually fuel your delicate, burning ego. The love you feel for yourself turns to pain when people withhold their praise and turn away from you because you are unpleasant to be with.

If you were to describe yourself, you would use words like beautiful or handsome, accomplished, clever, gifted, superior and extraordinary. If others were to describe you they would accuse you of bragging and label you conceited and full of yourself.

If your need for admiration and fawning attention is denied, you become even more agitated. Impatience and then unreasonable rage can follow.

How do you recognize the beginnings and growth of Narcissistic Personality Disorder within yourself?

A clue is that you demand to have the best of everything, whether it is a table in a restaurant, service at a dry cleaner, or a new car or golf club.

You are extremely thin-skinned about taking any criticism whatsoever. If pushed into a corner, you will betray others to save yourself. You do not know the meaning of fair play or loyalty. You will constantly belittle others to bolster your own ego.

A lot of the time you feel insecure and a bit ashamed of what you are, and that makes you angry. You fill yourself with rage and contempt for others, or slowly fall into a state of depression.

The Diagnostic and Statistical Manual of Mental Disorders (DSM-5) of the American Psychiatric Association sets out the criteria for the diagnosis of a number of mental conditions.

For Narcissistic Personality Disorder, they suggest you may have the disorder if you experience any of the following symptoms:

- You believe you are much more important than you are.
- You haven't achieved anything special, but you feel you should be recognized as being superior over others.
- In social exchanges, you are extremely boastful, greatly exaggerating your talents and accomplishments.
- You spend many of your waking hours day-dreaming or fantasizing about beauty,

brilliance, success and power or even the perfect mate for you.

- You often think you are intellectually alone on this planet. You believe intrinsically that you are smarter than everyone around you and nobody can really understand you except another equally gifted individual.
- You need to be admired like other people need to eat and drink.
- You believe that you are entitled to the best of everything and the undying admiration of others.
- You expect you will receive special favors just for being you.
- You believe that people will automatically comply with your wishes and expectations.
- You have no qualms whatsoever about using other people to accomplish what you want.
- You are incapable of discerning and disinterested in meeting the needs and feelings of other people.
- You envy others and are convinced that those who meet you envy you.
- Your behavior is full of arrogance and your body language is haughty.

In other words, your behavior is the antithesis of what is needed to make friends and influence people.

If your behavior matches most the symptoms listed above, or even if it matches most and you feel incredibly sad most of the time, the good news is that your disorder can be successfully treated and you can return to a normal life.

Talk to your doctor or mental health provider and explore options for treatment. Many of these remedies can be done on your own and at home, and we will discuss a number of them later in this book.

A lesser form of narcissism is egocentrism and we will discuss it briefly before we move further.

To either a small or a large extent, we all see our worlds with ourselves at the center. We ask "what's in it for me?" when considering an employment contract or a business deal. Many of us keep an informal mental scorecard to determine if our relationships are worth keeping. Are we expending more energy and resources on a person who is returning nothing of value to our lives?

Only the very wise and mature can grow past basic egocentrism and see the world through larger eyes, through the eyes of many other people.

Swiss psychologist Jean Piaget conducted a number of research studies into our inherent egocentrism and its impact on us at different stages of our lives. He illustrated how young children rarely possess the ability to see the world from any other perspective than their own.

As people grow and mature in their personalities, however, they learn to consider another person's point of view. They are able to imagine what the other person might be going through during a difficult time. Parents often become extremely intuitive and empathetic about their children, understanding before words are spoken how a series of events can impact the child they love.

But we are still locked into our own view of the world in many other areas of our lives. We find it hard to understand why friends take actions that we think are foolish, or why our bosses make moves we consider to be ill-considered. We are looking at our friends' lives and our boss's world from our own perspectives.

When we feel embarrassed, we are practicing egocentrism. We believe that everyone is watching us make a mistake, never realizing that most people are so wrapped up in their own egocentricisms that they believe everyone is watching them instead.

You are being egocentric when you jump ahead of people in lines, when you take the parking spot another person had signaled they were moving into, and when you take more than your share of cookies on a plate.

Being habitually late is a form of egocentrism. You believe that your time and what is happening to you is more important than the lives and time of all the people waiting for you.

You are looking after your needs, and are not too worried about those of the people around you.

Most of us feel a little bad when we practice acts of egocentrism and we make efforts to be more considerate of others in the future. We police ourselves, and gradually, we grow our personalities into broader areas, where we see the world from the perspective of others as well as our own.

But sometimes we do not. Our lack of empathy for others just grows. We start to care less and less about the needs of others.

You begin to have more difficulty understanding other people's opinions. Sometimes you even have trouble grasping reality the way it is, especially when it conflicts with what they see.

Gradually, over time, your egocentricity starts sliding more and more in the direction of full-fledged narcissism.

In the next two chapters, we will look further into additional traits and signs of narcissists and persons with Narcissistic Personality Disorder. After that, we will look at a number of aspects of life to determine how narcissism cuts a destructive path across your personal relationships, your workplace success, and your ability to lead a healthy and fulfilling life.

In each instance, we will look at solutions to overcoming narcissism and regaining a balanced personality.

Chapter 2: How to identify whether or not you are a narcissist

American humorist Dave Barry once said that when there is trouble around us and things look bad, there is always somebody who has a solution and is willing to take command.

"Very often, that individual is crazy," he writes.

Looking through the colorful history of our world, his humor takes on a serious note. It appears as if he could be right.

Narcissists such as Adolph Hitler, Joseph Stalin and Angel of Death Joseph Mengele are all examples of the terrible toll unchecked narcissism can take on innocent people. When your self-love rises to the point that you believe you are right and everyone around you is even less than human, violence and chaos will reign if you assume any position of power.

Understanding the true nature of narcissism is complicated, however. Sometimes full-blown narcissistic behavior is less evil; it manifests itself in the silliness of demands for attention and worship by movie stars and quasi-celebrities.

Either way, the quest to determine what makes a narcissist and to figure out if you are one is an interesting journey.

Many great philosophers and psychologists have struggled with the question throughout the ages.

Back in 1923, Austrian-born Israeli Jewish philosopher Martin Buber thought he had figured it out. In his ground-breaking book *Ich und Du,* (I-Thou and I-It), he first explores the I-Thou relationships, the real relationships. These include relationships like two lovers, a person and a pet, and even two strangers meeting on a train. He then looks at the I-It relationship where the beings do not meet. The "I" in this case is just an idea, a part of an individual mind. It is a relationship of one.

In the Ich-Es relationship, the I-it, only one person matters and that is the self. It is a relationship of yourself with yourself. Other people are just objects to be used an experience.

Buber's look into the narcissistic personality was followed by a number of other explanations, culminating in 2003 with the publication of *Why Is It Always About You? The Seven Deadly Sins of Narcissism* by clinical social worker and therapist Sandy Hotchkiss.

The seven sins of narcissism, which could equally be described as the seven clues that you have become a narcissist, included shamelessness, magical thinking, arrogance, envy, entitlement, exploitation and bad boundaries.

In this chapter and the next, we are going to provide a series of tests and clues to help you determine if you are (a) a narcissist and (b) if you have developed full-blown Narcissistic Personality Disorder.

Before we can talk about effective change and at home therapies, we first need to know your reality when it comes to the degree of your feelings of self and self-worth.

Here are seven questions to answer honestly to determine if your narcissism is getting past the point of normally healthy self-love and respect.

1. Can you be generous without being recognized?

Let's pretend that it is the holiday season of giving to those less fortunate and a local charity contacts you for assistance. They need someone with brains and connections to lead the annual drive to gather more than 10,000 turkeys and $10,000 to help the poor families in your community.

You have the time and energy to run the turkey drive, and you have the personal bank account to donate the $10,000 without any problem whatsoever.

You agree to help.

But, do you insist that your name personally be attached to the turkey drive? Do you agree to give the money but insist that the organization agree to a specified number of mentions including a newspaper article and photo? Do you demand a thank-you ad containing your photo and name?

It is a misconception that narcissistic people are mean. In fact, many of them are outlandishly generous. But when they give, they want to receive back immediately in attention and public accolades.

2. Can you actually put the needs of someone else ahead of your own?

Let's picture a night that you come home from work exhausted. You've been fighting a cold and your energy is depleted. To make matters worse, this was deadline day for a major project. You ended up going in to work two hours earlier than normal, and working two hours later.

You have just made a bit of supper and settled down to eat it when the phone rings. Your neighbor, and good friend, needs your help.

A single mom, she has one child who must go to a doctor's clinic down the street. The little one is running a high fever and the other is really frightened. She asks if you can pop over to her place and babysit her other child, who is already asleep in bed.

You know she has nobody else to ask.

If you're response is, "No, I'm too tired," you are a narcissist.

If you gather your supper, put a little foil wrap over it and trudge to the neighbor's house, you are a genuine friend. You are able to put the very real emergency of a friend over your own self interests.

But if you look after yourself and your tiredness first, even though it may be understandable, it is still narcissistic.

3. Are you capable of listening?

A co-worker is speaking to you about his concerns. A new corporate policy has been put in place that will impact everyone's health benefits and he is deeply worried that he will not be able to pay for dental work that his children need.

You see his lips moving, and you hear his voice.

But your mind is miles away. You are figuring out if the changes mean that you can still deduct your gym membership from the company coffers.

He talks on and on, and you nod. But really, you are just waiting for him to stop for air so you can pipe in about your gym membership. Really, that's the most important thing, isn't it?

His kids can get braces when they are older. You can't be concerned about that.

Come to think of it, this conversation is pretty typical for you. When other people are talking, you are just waiting for them to finish so you can talk about yourself and how whatever happening is impacting you and your life.

You feel annoyed when they just don't stop talking, and then contemptuous of their opinions.

Most of the time when you start to respond, your sentence begins with the word "but."

Whatever the topic of conversation is at the moment, you inevitably find a way to link it back to you.

You are walking down a corridor and there is a lovely painting hanging on the wall. A colleague remarks on its beauty. You look at it and respond "I painted a scene just like that once," or "I actually have that print, but I got tired of looking at it."

Whatever illness someone else starts to tell you about, you respond by letting them know you had it and worse. Whatever project they are working on, you advise that you have done that, and better. Whatever item they have purchased, you make it clear you have one and yours is more expensive or at least nicer.

Every conversation inevitably leads right back to you. And even while you appear to be listening, all you are doing is waiting for air time to move right in and center the talk back on you and your life.

4. You cannot take any kind of criticism.

You finish breakfast and leave the table to get ready for your day. When you are dressed and ready to leave for work, your spouse gently says: "I wonder if you would mind putting your breakfast dishes in the dishwasher when you are finished eating. If we all do that, I won't be late for work trying to tidy everything before I go."

You fly into a rage.

"I had one little bowl and a cup and you don't love me enough to put it in the dishwasher for me? How much more am I supposed to be doing around here? I have such a horrible work day ahead of me, that I cannot believe that you would pick this of all mornings to criticize me and tell me I needed to do still more!"

You storm out of the house and drive extremely aggressively all the way to work. You are still steaming when you arrive at your desk. You tell a co-worker about how unreasonable your spouse is.

You feel the weight of the world on your shoulders. You feel unloved and un-appreciated. Even when your spouse calls later to apologize, you still unleash a barrage of words about the pain and injustice you have endured over this terrible criticism.

It takes a few more days and flowers and a gift from your spouse to put things right again.

5. You cannot play by the rules.

If the traffic light is red, but you can't see any other cars around, you always go through the light. If the road says "no trespassing" you assume that means everyone except you. You are the person that has to be rescued from the flooded road because you went through the barricade, not believing you could be so inconvenienced as to have to find another route.

You jump ahead of others in the grocery line and the traffic queues. You park in the handicapped spot because the day is cold and it's closer to the door.

The company says you can have one coffee mug, so you take two, one for your desk and one for your home.

Whatever the rule is, you have to bend it or break it. Even if it is something silly that you don't really care about, you still have to prove to yourself each time you encounter it that it is for other people, not you.

With every decision you make to break the rule, you cause inconvenience and annoyance to others, but you don't really care. Tough on them!

If they are too stupid to break the rules themselves, why should you wait for them? If they want to stand in a line all day and wait, that's their problem, not yours.

6. When you have a falling out with friends or a loved one, it is never your fault.

You have lots of friends, but not too many old friends. That is because sooner or later all people disappoint you. They do things to you that break the relationship. You can't really trust people to do the right thing, after all. They will let you down sooner or later.

No matter what happens to cause friction in your relationships it is never your fault. You forgot to pick them up to go to the cinema as promised and they waited half an hour in the cold? Well, what did they expect? They didn't call you after work to remind you. And besides, they picked a show you didn't even want to see. You were just going to do a favor to go with them, and this is the thanks you get? You're a bit late and they're upset with you? How unfair is that.

You had a live-in love for a few months and then one day you had a huge fight and they moved out. And it was all because they wanted you to go to their sister's funeral with them. But you hate death and funerals. You don't ask them to go places with you that they hate, although you can't remember what it is that they hate enough that they wouldn't go with you when you asked.

Or maybe they wanted to move to a new town so they didn't have to drive two hours a day to get to work. But even though you weren't working at the time, you didn't want to make the move. Moving is such a bother and you really did like your apartment. So they wanted to make a federal case about it, just because they had to do four extra hours of driving a day? Really! If they loved you, they would have happily done that.

7.   Your charm drives people to you; your self-centeredness carries them away.

You are good looking and intelligent. You have a brilliant smile and a quick word and insincere compliment for everyone who crosses your path. People call you a natural salesperson and are drawn to you immediately.

Your self-confidence oozes out of you at social gatherings. You are the person they would most like to be with. They use terms like suave and sexy and exciting to describe you.

It is only when they get to know you that they realize you are also prone to outlandish anger and extreme moods. The veneer wears off quickly.

Your anger is triggered by even the slightest criticism or even the slightest suggestion of expected behavior or control.

You like to golf, and on sunny summer weekends, you want to be on the course without fail. But your spouse advises there are weekends coming up and they want to alter your routine. You have to travel to another city to attend a wedding and they'd like you to participate in a family camping weekend just as the school break starts.

What is this? Someone is trying to totally control your life. You will show them. You rage and rant and decide to golf even more rather than less. Let them take the kids and go camping without you.

While they are gone, you will even charm and bed someone who has more appreciation for your charms and talents. You deserve more than to be controlled by someone who says they love you. You will show them!

If the affair is discovered, it is clearly their fault, not yours. They weren't thinking about what you wanted at all. You had no choice but to seek comfort elsewhere.

How do you score yourself?

If you have done even one of these things, you have behaved badly. It might have been a lapse in judgment and you may have felt bad afterwards and determined to be more sensitive and mature in the future.

But if you have recognized yourself in two or more of these scenarios, you are exhibiting narcissistic behavior. If you or some aspect of you is visible in all of them, your behavior is seriously narcissistic and you need to consider some kind of intervention or therapy.

You can help yourself unless you are in the seriously advanced stages of narcissism and need professional therapy.

For the average narcissist, however, recognizing your tendency to think only of yourself is a good square one.

You didn't develop those unpleasant behaviors overnight and you won't be able to just snap your fingers and get rid of them.

But you will be able to set out a course of small steps to move you back to more normally accepted behavior that will enrich your life and the lives of those around you.

Before we work on those changes, let us do one more chapter of soul-searching.

There is a difference between narcissistic behavior and full-fledged Narcissistic Personality Disorder.

Let us now look at the symptoms marking that disorder in the next chapter and determine whether or not your narcissism has augmented to being a personality disorder.

Chapter 3: Do you suffer from Narcissistic Personality Disorder?

In one of the greatest literary put-downs of all time, author George Eliot once described a character as being so full of himself that "He was like the cock who thought the sun had risen to hear him crow."

We have all met that man or some semblance of him, the person whose self-love is boundless. Some of us have worked for him and understood that no amount of fawning admiration could possibly feed the hunger his heart needed.

We have read stories of aging movie stars with their prestige slowly sinking and their faces deeply lined still demanding to be adored by a series of younger, sometimes paid, lovers.

We all need to be loved and admired, but when our need becomes all-encompassing and totally out of balance with our realities, we may be suffering from Narcissistic Personality Disorder.

As with all personality disorders, the American Psychiatric Association provides a checklist of criteria before a diagnosis can be made. While a professional therapist is needed for a formal diagnosis, we can use that readily available criteria and apply it to familiar situations to help you determine if a reasonable assumption could be made that you had the disorder or were bordering on it.

Health experts at The Mayo Clinic describe Narcissistic Personality Disorder as a mental disorder that manifests itself when you have a vastly inflated sense of your own importance.

We all need admiration, but when you have NPD you have a need for it that exceeds normality. Conversely, you have no empathy for the people around you.

You appear to be super self-confident but that is a mask. Behind it, your self-esteem is incredibly fragile. It is like a mental eggshell, so delicate that the slightest criticism can shatter it and make it almost impossible to put it back together again.

This hunger for admiration, lack of empathy for others, and total inability to take any criticism does not add up to an easy life.

You will have severe problems making any relationships prosper, being able to do purposeful, meaningful work either by yourself or with others, and even in achieving financial stability.

In some cases, you may be able to use your inflated ego to charm your way to power or a top leadership role, but yours is the original unhappy head that bears the crown. You will never be pleased with what you have accomplished and the more successful you are, the more prone you will be to criticism, which will ultimately destroy you.

Having NPD is no prescription for a happy life. It is just the opposite, a vehicle that carries you down a dead-end road of disappointment.

You will never be able to feed your ego with sufficient amounts of admiration; your lack of empathy will grow and fester into outright contempt for others, and your relationships, so exciting in the beginning, are doomed and you will likely end up all alone or with a long-suffering partner who hates you but for their own weakness, lacks the resources to leave you.

It is not a pretty picture of a life well lived, but it is a treatable disorder and you have the power to change. That is the positive part of the equation.

There are diverging opinions on what exactly causes NPD with the most commonly held idea being that it stems from our childhood when parents overdid the idea of positive reinforcement.

Instead of being quietly reassuring of their children, these parents went to the extreme of excessive pampering. Sometimes parents, lacking in talent and esteem in their own right, move the burden or super-achieving onto the shoulders of their children, causing the youngster to feel they must be super-accomplished and superior to be loved.

But that does not explain the other end of the spectrum where people emerge with NPD from extremely poor and abusive childhoods. They may build a fantasy world in which they are admired and loved and extremely accomplished to deal with the darkness of their own reality.

The signs of NPD first become evident around the time a child turns into a teenager and gathers strength throughout adolescence.

Instead of diminishing with the years, as the person actually starts to make their way in the world and accomplish things, the NPD begins to grow even more powerful until gradually, it takes over the person's personality and their entire world.

How do you know if you suffer from NPD?

The characteristics mentioned above manifest themselves in a variety of ways.

Have you ever been on a vacation where you met another person and to hear him talk, you clearly got the impression he was the most important person in a huge corporation? This person seems to know everything that is happening in the firm. He has little insights into business giants his company has dealt with. Yet despite his apparent power and prestige, here he sits with his feet up, enjoying himself at a fabulous resort. You envy him.

A few months later, through some series of serendipitous circumstances, you meet them in their real life and their real environment. They may in fact work at the company they discussed with you, but they are a maintenance man there, handling important papers only when they are shredded into the trash. Their brushes with business giants come from parking their cars, and the luxury vacation came from a ticket they bought in a church lottery.

You may dismiss the janitor as a con artist or just an outright liar, but chances are, he is suffering from NPD.

When you have this disorder, you often have a grandiose sense of your own importance. If you are that janitor, you may actually believe that you are the pivot around which the big company operates.

When you meet other people, you exaggerate your achievements and talents. You expect to be recognized as a star, even though your light has never shone on any great accomplishment.

Do you dream during the day as much as at night? When you close your eyes or just remove your focus from what is really happening, do you repeatedly see yourself standing on stage, dressed in designer clothing, clasping a coveted award? Do you hear yourself standing before the podium, delivering an address that stirs all those nameless, faceless people to leap to their feet in riotous applause?

Perhaps it is not only your accomplishments they are honoring. Are they naming you one of the most beautiful people on the planet? Does your elegant face shine out from a back-lit billboard behind you as you speak?

Or perhaps you are winning the presidency of your country? Are your loyal campaign managers raising your arms and encouraging the audience to shout your name, over and over, on an endless sea of love and support?

How does it really feel to have the fate of the world in your hands? You know; you were there. You have seen and done it all in your daydreams.

When you wake up in the morning and prepare for your day, do you know instinctively that you are special? Are you absolutely comfortable in knowing that you are by far the smartest person in your house, in your workplace, in your circle of friends and in your neighborhood?

You could go a little further, couldn't you? If those in charge would just ask, you could tell them how to solve the big challenges they are facing. It's clear to you which road to take.

Perhaps you should find new friends. Yours are holding you down. They are so slow-thinking. You would feel more comfortable if you could find smarter, more accomplished friends.

Do you have a hunger to be admired that is never satiated? Do you need to hear at home that you look amazing today? When you arrive at the office, do you expect that the report you presented yesterday will be held up as an example of the best report of its type ever to be presented in the history of the company?

Should you not have the biggest office with the nicest furnishings? Shouldn't your car be in the prime spot closest to the door? Why should you have to make do with a second-hand computer? You deserve the absolute best of everything and you know it. You are entitled to it. Nobody deserves it more than you.

Are you curt with the doorman or the receptionist? They are beneath your attention, cogs in the wheel there merely to help your day go right so you can super-achieve as always.

A co-worker wants to talk? You don't. Close the door. Who are these people who want to hound you with stupid stories of their stupid lives? Don't they know you need all your brain power to super achieve?

Well, there's Ron or Jennie. You will let them in. They are bringing tea, telling you how great you look today, telling you how super cool you were at the last board meeting, telling you the fall-out from your proposal is stupendous. They are really thick, but at least they have some idea of how important you are. They can find their way into your inner sanctum.

Ron or Jennie tells you that Andy or Sue has a great idea that will make the company get a big public relations boost when it is really needed. They are hoping to get in today to talk to you about it. It really is a good idea. You bring them in right away and charm all the details right out of them. You assure them you will take it forward to the right ears for them.

You take your new idea forward. What do you mean that it was someone else's idea? Of course not. They may have brought up something, but you were already thinking about that and you were just being polite listening to how they thought it could work. You can make it work brilliantly. They couldn't.

Your boss loves your new idea. It's all good.

But they think some office staff has to be laid off ...you have to get rid of either Ron or Jennie. No problem, let them go...I mean, how hard is it to find someone who can bring you coffee?

Back in your office a collection is being taken up for Joe whose kid has cancer and needs some kind of operation that insurance doesn't cover.

You say no. They need to change the system. Paying from your own pocket isn't going to solve anything. Who cares? You have new projects to work on.

Your personality function is impaired as the day goes on. Sometimes you feel on top of the world, in charge of everything, and a few minutes later, you feel desperately lacking in confidence.

You are regulated only by the admiration others show for you. Your whole sense of self-worth is wrapped up by what others outside of yourself think of you and the behaviors they exhibit towards you. You are becoming a shell, sustained only by the cushion of support from others. You need more of that, more admiration, more recognition.

Your personal standards are impossibly high because you believe you are exceptional. Or, sometimes even within the same day, they are impossibly low because whether or not you lift a finger, you are entitled to a big office, a big salary and a big life.

You are antagonistic to others and have no empathy for them or their concerns. Your world totally revolves around you and only you.

That is what makes having any kind of relationship so difficult. People consistently disappoint you when you let them close. You really don't care about them anyhow, and inevitably, they get tired of your endless need for admiration and your lack of genuine caring for them.

This keeps most relationships superficial. They are there just to temporarily heighten your self-esteem. You do not need all these people when they want you; just when you want them. Why don't they just understand that and deal with it better?

Sometimes, in the evenings especially, when your thoughts do move to other people, you are deeply jealous of them. How does Dave deserve to have a house and a cottage? That lazy, stupid guy never did an honest day's work in his life.

And somebody said Kathy is pulling in six figures now? Selling real estate? Can't be ….must all be a smokescreen. She's too dumb to do that. I wouldn't buy a shed from her!

Then you settle into a more comfortable frame of mind, thinking of all the other people who must be deeply jealous of you. You are so good-looking, intelligent, and accomplished, they all wish they had a piece of you. Dream on!

If these scenarios make up portions of your days, you likely have NPD. We say likely, because while it is an accepted mental disorder, it is still extremely difficult to fully diagnose.

Unlike a physical illness, you cannot have a simple blood test and determine positively or negatively if you are suffering from this disorder.

If you seek professional help, your therapist will take you through a series of diagnostic tests to ensure that your symptoms match those on the accepted criteria.

But deep down, if you recognize yourself in most of the above scenarios, it is time to consider the possibility that you have this disorder and to start to take steps to re-balance your personality for a healthier and happier life.

We are ready now to take our discussion on narcissism further, to look at how it impacts many aspects of our life and how we can make changes to control it.

In the next chapter, we will look at how narcissism strains our personal relationships with others and what we can do to start rebuilding meaningful friendships and intimate relationships.

Chapter 4: How narcissism impacts your ability to relate to others

American aphorist Mason Cooley once remarked that if you withhold admiration from a narcissist, you will be disliked. But if you give it, you will be treated with indifference.

That certainly doesn't build much of a basis for any deep and lasting relationships.

In fact, people with narcissism and Narcissistic Personality Disorder often end their days all alone because the people who once genuinely loved them just can't reach them anymore.

Furthermore, the total lack of reciprocal caring on the part of the narcissist takes its toll over time and finally, in a desperate bid to restore their own self-identity, the partner leaves.

In this chapter, we will look at relationships first from the point of view of the narcissist, and secondly, from the point of view of their spouses and children. Narcissism affects all relationships, including friendships, but when a person becomes too difficult, most friends will simply just avoid the person.

The problem comes for those who are tied to them in marriage or because they are a father or mother. Escape and avoidance is not so easy in such circumstances, but there are some steps that can be taken to handle the relationship better.

A number of scientific studies have been conducted into the impact of narcissism on relationships. Two in particular give us insight into better understanding the relationship from the narcissist's point of view.

A 2002 study called "Does self-love lead to love for others? A story of narcissistic "game playing" published in the *Journal of Personality and Social Psychology* found researchers compiling five studies that investigated the links among narcissism, self-esteem and love.

Completed by researchers W. Keith Campbell, Craig A. Foster and Eli J. Finkel, the study saw that in all cases, narcissism was associated primarily with a game-playing love style.

Narcissists play games in their relationships because of their intense need for power and autonomy. They have less of a commitment to their relationships than those unaffected with narcissism.

At the same time, the narcissist may also engage in what the researchers called "manic love," as in a series of one-night stands designed to boost their own self esteem.

A second study shed more light on the potential of a narcissist in a relationship by showing that many narcissists are actually aware of their condition, even though they seem helpless to fix it.

In a ground-breaking study published in *PLOS One,* Professor Brad Bushman at Ohio State University and his team discovered that a single question appears to be extremely effective in identifying a true narcissist.

The question, which is one in a diagnostic test of 40 questions, asks this:

"To what extent do you agree with this statement: I am a narcissist?"

(For the purposes of the study, narcissist was defined as egotistical, vain and self-focused.)

The responders were asked to pick a number between 1 and 7, with 1 meaning not very true of me and 7 meaning very true of me.

Those who picked 7 or a number very close to it were in fact narcissists, based on their answers to the other questions. So in other words, they knew they were narcissists.

Bushman, who co-authored the paper, wrote that narcissists do not have a problem admitting they are narcissist. They believe they deserve special treatment and they don't try to hide that expectation.

If you are a narcissist, and yet a part of you yearns for a spouse, children and the stability of a real relationship, how can you overcome your own condition enough to create that relationship?

It comes down to recognizing your narcissism, which we now know is technically possible, and working to silence your inner voice that is so critical of the world around you in an effort to build yourself up.

We all work throughout our lives to challenge behaviors and attitudes that are destructive in our lives, and the narcissist is no different.

If you are a narcissist, you may be able to successfully improve a relationship by practicing a technique known as Voice Therapy.

This is tough. But rarely is anything about change easy.

Voice Therapy as a treatment for narcissism is all about silencing some of the inner voices that fuel our over-exaggerated sense of self entitlement and self-importance.

As a narcissist, just like everyone else, you are clinging to your "stories" that drive your behavior. You demand to be treated special because you were deprived as a child, for example. You hold tight to that story, because in your cloudy thinking, it justifies everything that you do. It races through your head at the oddest times, reinforcing that you deserve the best now, that you can take without asking, that you can show disregard for others because of the disregard that was shown to you.

Your parents may have been emotionally cold, and you now exhibit emotional coldness in return, a justification for your suffering as a child who wanted to be cuddled and loved. You cling to your story, all the while pushing away those who would love you now, happier instead to hold tight to your story.

With Voice Therapy, you try to silence your story, or even better, to change it. When you start at the core of your behavior and change its whole justification, it makes other changes easier to accomplish.

You may have grown up being compared negatively to a superstar sibling or to other people's children. Now you spend hours endlessly comparing yourself to others, envying them or being contemptuous of them. You are superior to them, you know that.

But what if you changed your inner voice? What if you changed your story and didn't have to measure your self-worth compared to others? How could that change your behavior?

Voice Therapy is an excellent way to start the process of change to build better relationships.

Another technique that is often effective in the self-help mode is to practice Self-Caring rather than self-esteem. There is a subtle difference between self-caring and self-love. With the former, you are permitted to do acts of kindness for yourself, to stop endlessly striving and endlessly comparing yourself.

You can sometimes let your wall down and realize that you are human after all. You do not need to be perfect in the eyes of others and more important still, you do not have to be perfect in the eyes of yourself.

Instead of instinctively protecting yourself as an act of survival, you can consciously care for yourself as an act of concern. Your care for yourself becomes a positive, something you build on to express real, genuine love, not a grasping things away from others kind of love.

As an example of how Self-Caring can work, you begin to keep a daily agenda of accomplishments. You already know how you exaggerate in front of other people about your accomplishments, always making yourself sound grander and more important than you really are in the total scheme of things.

But each day, you actually do accomplish things, good and important things in your life. If you make a record of them, a kind of accomplishment journal, you will start to feel an authenticity to your claims. You might think that would fuel your exaggeration and make it even worse, but the opposite happens. Instead, you start to believe at a deeper level that you really do accomplish things, and you become more at peace with yourself.

Both Voice Therapy and Self-Caring techniques are difficult and gradual processes. Sometimes you only start to look at ways to handle your narcissism when your loved one threatens to leave if you don't change.

It will actually be more successful if you recognize your own unhappiness first and start the process of change on your own. You like autonomy; you like to be in control of yourself. If it is your decision to make a difference in your story, and to kindly recognize your own real accomplishments, the change will inevitably be more lasting and more effective.

What happens if you are the person who falls in love with a narcissist?

Before you can start a process of working to change them or even end the relationship, it is a good idea to consider what you found attractive about this person so full of self-love in the first place?

There are many reasons people fall in love with a narcissist, not the least being that many of them are utterly charming when you first meet them.

But what else was in their personality that attracted you? Were you the child of a narcissistic parent and were attracted by the familiarity of it? Do you think normal relationships require constantly giving admiration?

Are you not inclined to make your own decisions and control your own life? Do you prefer a passive role and does that make you vulnerable to those who would wish to control you?

Is your self-esteem so wrecked that your partner's frequent criticism of you rings true? Do you think this is all you really deserve in a relationship?

Many people who fall into relationships with narcissists and stay with them, despite lack of fulfillment coupled with the presence of physical or mental abuse, do so because they are too lacking in self-love that they think this is okay.

It is important to figure out your motivation for getting involved with the narcissist before you even begin to try to change your partner or yourself. Otherwise, you will simply walk away from one narcissist and likely end up living with another a few months later, still seeking someone else to complete a part of you that is not mature or developed.

If you are the spouse of a narcissist, you may have developed a keen understanding of your partner's personality disorder, and are even compassionate about their lack of self-esteem that leads them to self-promotion on a grand scale.

If you decide to take that route, you must be fully confident in yourself first. If you do not totally understand and believe that you are equal to your partner and that you deserve a fulfilling relationship, you will not have sufficient power to start to change them.

If you fail to find your own self-confidence and instead keep trying to please your narcissistic spouse, you are in danger of becoming a victim of emotional, verbal, sexual or physical abuse and ending up seriously injured and emotionally drained from the experience.

In extreme cases, you may not be safe under any circumstances and must flee the relationship to survive.

If you just endure and fall into the victim role, you will end up both physically and emotionally hurt from the experience. In that case, it is not love but a case of co-dependency with the narcissist, and it has no happy ending.

Loving a narcissist is not a relationship to take lightly. You do not have to be a victim, and you may even be able to establish the basis of a semi-reasonable relationship. But that takes great confidence and strength on your part.

You may also decide to just leave, and that too takes strength and is understandable.

As a general rule, the full-fledged narcissist is more apt to be more emotionally and verbally abusive than physically abuse, although there are always exceptions.

The narcissist's need for power and control is often fed by their ability to belittle and control you. They remind you of how little you are worth, that your presence in the world is insignificant, and that you would be nothing without your relationship with them.

Life with a narcissist means they will diminish your abilities, your looks and your talents, all to keep you in control, to make sure that you never attain enough confidence to leave.

Sexually, narcissists demand that you submit to their wishes. As with all things in the relationship, it is all about them.

If you give in to the narcissist's never ending demands, if you stoke the fire of their self-admiration endlessly, if you sacrifice all that is you just to please them, you will still never make them happy and you will destroy yourself in the process.

If you become financially or emotionally dependent on them, you will rarely successfully escape from their clutches.

You may harbor a dream that someday they will wake up and appreciate who you are and all that you do for them, but they are totally incapable of that sentiment. It will not happen. They will also have new demands; they will always keep raising the bar for what is expected.

A narcissist may stay with you for many years, even a lifetime, if they feel their needs are being met, but they will never appreciate you or make any effort to make you happy. They think just being with them is enough.

In the average relationship involving a narcissist, there is a lot of drama, a lot of fighting and a lack of genuine love.

The narcissistic partner will make all the family decisions and they will all revolve around them and how it works for them. If one of their decisions turns disastrous, they will blame everyone else.

If the narcissist develops other behavioral programs, such as alcoholism or a gambling addiction, it will always be somebody else's fault, never their own.

You are the primary person who will be blamed. They will also blame children, setting up a destructive cycle for their own children to be unloved and under-appreciated, so that they in turn may turn into narcissists for survival's sake.

The problems of relationships with narcissists can usually not be contained behind closed doors either. They will behave outlandishly at family or public gathering, picking fights, saying nasty things to relatives, and burning bridges in all directions.

The narcissist's tendency to use others for their own needs and then discard them breaks down friendships, family structures and community regard.

If you want to change a narcissist's behavior, and they are not physically abusive, you have to first change your own way of dealing with them. (If they are physically abusive, you cannot start these steps without placing yourself in considerable danger. Do not attempt to discuss behavior issues with an abusive narcissist.)

If you believe you can get through, and you have another family member willing to be with you, start by saying calmly and clearly that certain behavior is not okay.

Be careful how you phrase this. Do not start by saying "You are being ...." because that is a direct criticism that will lead only to defensiveness and rage.

Use the "I" approach instead of the "you" approach. You can say "I was upset at Carol's wedding when you said the groom was an idiot. I was embarrassed."

The narcissist may just say "okay" and that might be the beginning of change. If instead they challenge you and say "what do you expect me to do about it? He is an idiot," again answer with the "I" approach.

"I do not expect anything now and I respect your opinion. I would just ask that you not voice such an opinion again at a family gathering like that."

Or, you could use a bit of humor to soften the conversation, but this gets your point across.

You could say:

"I couldn't argue that he isn't an idiot (with a smile), but I'd just be more comfortable if you just didn't say it in your outside voice at family gatherings."

If you get through that small exercise without a major blow-up, continue to react calmly to your narcissistic spouse. Think about how to phrase your words so as to not make them look like a direct attack.

As you gradually spread out your boundaries, the next step is to try to arrange for your narcissist to get needed treatment.

Despite their disorder, narcissists can be treated and they can change. The problem is that because the narcissist believes they are perfect and the problem is with everyone else, it is difficult to get them to see a therapist.

That does not mean it is impossible. Sometimes the narcissistic spouse can be lured in by the other partner under the guise of marriage counseling that will "include some private sessions."

At other times, with the marriage in crisis, the narcissist may feel the beginning of self-awareness, the uneasy notion that something is wrong but they know it is not their fault. Even if they are brought to the therapist feeling they are coming to fix something someone else has broken, it is still a good first step.

The next step is helping the narcissist to adopt a more realistic perception of his or her personality. This evolves slowly, with the help of the therapist, the spouse, a parent or a sibling.

As a spouse, you help your narcissistic partner court reality by refusing to give in to their unrealistic portrait of themselves. You tell them occasionally that what they want to do is not acceptable, and that their behavior is not okay.

Therapy will be less effective if the narcissist is not making a genuine effort to change. If the therapist is mocked, threatened, and belittled, the impact will obviously be less impactful than if the narcissist admits, like an addict, that they have a problem and need to change.

If you are a narcissist and you do want to change so that you can embrace more lasting and deeper relationships, this will be a difficult and disorienting time. The world as you know it, in all its dimensions, is crumbling around you and with it your ego and your entire sense of self. Can you rebuild your house of cards?

You may learn how to consciously control certain behaviors that make you more acceptable in your family. But you will always be vulnerable to returning to the old stories, the old behaviors and the old exaggerated sense of self. You have been clinging to it as your lifeline for so long, life without it is frightening.

You must tell yourself that you are still special, but you are becoming special in a new way, a way that will be more acceptable to the people around you. You also have an alibi for your despicable behavior in the family in the past: certain conditions of your past caused you to view the world in a way that was not healthful.

You will likely never acknowledge that you sustained a mental disturbance and still battle it every day. That would be just too much to accept. If you ever do acknowledge it, it is only to have something else to blame. None of what happened was your fault; you were sick. The sickness made you do it.

Whichever side you look at relationships, when there is a narcissist involved, there will be a challenge. What you must not do is constantly give in to hopelessness. Like many illnesses, NPD and narcissism can be treated and changes can be made.

But if you are being abused and are frightened, do not begin your stand for change alone. You could end up risking your life in the face of narcissistic rage.

Avoid challenging a narcissist when they are surrounded by their supporters (fawning co-workers, political volunteers, needy people who are clinging to their super-confidence). You will be in the minority position, and you will lose.

Be careful to keep all criticisms away from the narcissist's inner self and the characteristics they possess. They cannot accept any attack on their self and will fight to save themselves.

If they are yelling and threatening, do not respond in kind. As difficult as it is, stay calm. Escalating the fight will not end well, especially if they are more powerful than you.

Avoid feeding the narcissist's ego by serving up large portions of admiration daily and trying to secure concessions from them based on flattery. The narcissist will understand that you are weak and will take further advantage of you.

Sometimes, through fear of personal safety or of totally losing oneself, you must leave your marriage to a narcissist.

If you gather the courage to go, be very clear about one thing. You will receive no considerations whatsoever. Get a good lawyer, secure what is legally yours, and move on with your life. Do not expect the narcissist to feel sorrow or pain or any empathy for you. Remember, life is all about them, and this divorce will be another inconvenience in a life filled with many.

Try to walk away when you still have some decent memories of a life story. You will remember both the good and the bad parts; for the narcissist, there will be no recollection at all. It will just be done, gone like it never was. That is important to understand as you rebuild your life.

During the divorce, the narcissist will revert to true behavior, taking all that they can from you to benefit themselves. They will belittle you to friends and colleagues and even your children and steal as much of your money and personal possessions as they can get away with. Do everything possible to protect yourself.

The narcissistic spouse also cannot come to terms with the fact that they will no longer have complete influence and control over their ex, and they will try to regain it even if it means sacrificing the best interests of their children in the battle. Child support, shared parenthood and child visitation will be an unending challenge as each time they communicate, it will be an exercise in control.

It is more important than ever not to exhibit weakness at this time or easily give in to the first of what will end up being many unreasonable demands. Limit your responses to your narcissistic ex-spouse because every time you engage, they will seek to turn it to their advantage.

Try to remember, in the midst of the hurt and confusion, that the narcissist is not so much intent on hurting you as in protecting themselves. They want everything, they want admiration, and they want their own way. They will do whatever it takes to get it, and you are just a pawn in the game.

They will engage lawyers and use the court system shamelessly. Just when you think it is all settled and they will go away, they will trigger another battle. At some point, you will want to appeal to their basic goodness to just move on in life, but they cannot do that.

Remember, this is not your fault. You need to protect your own sense of value, mark your boundaries and do not allow them to be breached. That does not mean you need a battalion of lawyers and countersuits. Instead, it means refusing to respond to any communication that is abusive or disrespectful in nature. It is wisest, when dealing with a narcissist ex, to ensure that all communication between the two of you be done by email. At least then you have a record for the courts.

Do not threaten; do not respond to threats, and do not engage in anything but calm, written communication. Do not trade insult for insult. Instead, seek solutions. Get help with these communications from a professional third party if you are too emotionally battered to respond with calmness.

Build a support system around yourself but do not be surprised if even your best friends can hardly believe the lengths to which your ex will go to upset you.

When selecting a divorce lawyer, be sure that person has specifically had experience dealing with someone with NPD. That is the most vital choice you need to make, because without it, you cannot be adequately represented.

Chapter 5: The powerful force of narcissism in the workplace

Any discussion of narcissism in the workplace must contain some reference to Gordon Gekko, the fictional character in the movie *Wall Street*.

Michael Douglas won an Oscar for best actor for his role in the original 1987 film (there was a sequel made in 2010). That was the movie that gave the world the famous "greed" perspective on business, as in "greed, for lack of a better word, is good." Greed was portrayed as the essential ingredient for life, for money, for love and for knowledge.

Gekko also illustrated better than any description a Narcissistic Personality Disorder in the workplace.

He was vain, he insisted on always being right and thought everyone else was wrong. If he didn't directly benefit from an action, he didn't do it.

He didn't care who he threw under the bus when he had to blame someone. He turned on people without remorse or a second thought. He believed he was entitled to a world that was better than everyone else, with more money, more trappings of wealth and more beautiful sexual partners.

Gekko advocated greed for life, for money, for love and for knowledge as the essence of what fuels people.

Gekko's personality was textbook narcissism and a big screen example of Narcissistic Personality Disorder.

For the stressed-out workers around the world today, it is unfortunately not a rare sight.

According to Dr. Sam Vaknin, author of the book *Malignant Self Love – Narcissism Revealed,* between .7 and 1 percent of adults today suffer from NPD.

Unfortunately, the traits that ultimately destroy them are the very traits that make them corporate bosses and government leaders.

Michael Mcccoby, writing in *The Harvard Business Review* (January-February 2000), picked up on this trend when he assessed the traits of modern chief executive officers in the new millennium compared to their counterparts in the 1950s to 1980s.

Executives of the past were mainly quiet people who rarely courted the public spotlight and, if they had to speak in public, used statements carefully crafted by their professional public relations departments.

Contrast that to modern corporate giants like Bill Gates, the late Steve Jobs, Jeff Bezos and Jack Welch who jump in front of the spotlight, write their own books, and give off-the-cuff interviews where they expound on their personal philosophies on business and other things. They have become the corporate Gods and lesser leaders in smaller companies try to emulate them.

Boards of directors tend to hire and promote superstar managers. In troubled times, the person who promises the miracle is the savior.

As a result, at companies big and small throughout developed nations, we have a whole culture of managers who strive to become stars or "personalities" in their own right. Many of them take narcissistic tendencies. Their brimming self-confidence and charm is what the corporate world is eagerly seeking and they are quick to show that they can lead to the promised land of profit.

The new narcissistic CEOs believe that they can run the company better than anyone before them, and they could be right. Many are gifted; there are no laws that say mental disorders and high IQs can't inhabit the same brain.

The narcissist in business shows from the start that they don't really care whether everyone agrees with them or not; they will make things happen. Initially that is considered a great asset.

The narcissistic CEO may be a gifted, creative thinker, willing to take a risk and willing to terminate all those who do not jump on board their ship.

The problem is that sometimes (actually, quite often), the narcissistic leader can self-destruct and take the company down the road to disaster with them. Because they have demanded complete compliance and will tolerate no questioning of their action by the people around them, and have eliminated anyone who dares to disagree with them, nobody raises the alarm bell.

Even if co-workers secretly harbor doubts about the suitability of some corporate schemes, they keep their mouths shut for fear of losing their jobs.

Because narcissists often have great vision and can attract followers from the beginning, they grip control of the company firmly in their hands and as they go, so does the company. The problems start when their vision disengages from practical reality and their followers continue to walk blindly off the cliff behind them.

Working for a narcissist, even when you are part of the inner circle, is like playing with fire. That is because as the narcissist starts achieving real success, they become less and less grounded in reality and more and more convinced that they can do even more amazing feats. They are invincible.

They start to pay less and less attention to the people around them except to hear praise and admiration. When even the tiniest note of caution creeps in, they can turn on the employee and rid themselves of that person without a second thought. Loyalty and teamwork only goes one way with the narcissist, and that is to support them.

The higher narcissists climb, the less they are able to endure even the gentlest criticism. They are in place to execute their own ideas, to dominate meetings, and to make subordinates crumble in their wake. Instead of easing off a bit as they achieve one success after another, they become even more agitated and need even more admiration and total support.

Because narcissists have no empathy for other people, boards of directors hire them to do their "dirty work." Most people are bothered when they have to buy and sell companies, close stores and departments, and lay people off, but the narcissist doesn't have a second thought about it. The narcissist is seen as "tough" and that is an admirable quality when tough decisions have to be made.

The narcissist boss loves to ride roughshod over the board of directors because they consider all of them inferior to them. They also want all their employees to mirror exactly their thoughts about business.

If you are a narcissist, you will recognize yourself in the person described above. You may achieve greatness, but you must try to hold onto enough self-awareness to know when you are losing touch with reality.

Many narcissistic CEOs have trusted side-kicks, a vice-president or a personal assistant who they let close enough into their world to take minimal advice from. That has saved many of them from falling off the edge of self-love into self-destruction. Look around your workplace and see if there is someone you can court to be your sidekick. You will need them as they progress.

Maccoby coins the term "productive narcissists" to describe today's corporate leaders. They have an appetite for the public eye, they command a great deal of attention, and they announce grandiose schemes which normally work amazingly well.

The narcissist may actually be aware that their actions are outrageous on occasions, but that sentiment is immediately replaced by a re-interpretation of the experience. What we might consider just boorish behavior is dismissed by the practicing narcissist as an admirable trait.

"I don't suffer fools easily," they will proclaim, turning their rudeness into a positive trait in their eyes. They recognize their own brilliance and do not want to waste time discussing things with people who are decidedly inferior to them.

If you work in a company run by a narcissist, there is great potential for stress and unpleasantness.

Trademark narcissistic behavior includes rudeness and bullying which the narcissist interprets as the tools needed to do the job. They don't have time to coddle people, after all. This is the real world and if you can't stand the heat, get out of the kitchen. That is their ruling philosophy.

When narcissists lose their temper, it is because they were provoked and they needed to put a person in their place as an example to others. Every horrible behavior has some kind of justification.

What do you do if you end up working for a narcissist?

Rule number one if you want to stay employed is to never contradict them or disagree with them. They will turn on you so fast it will make your head spin and you will be out.

Do not engage them in any kind of chit-chat about your personal life. They will be affronted that you might think you are on the same level as they are. If they do not belittle you immediately, they will save the knowledge you offer and use it against you down the road.

Try to avoid saying outright compliments to them for fear you will have to come up with increasingly more fervent ones. Instead, look impressed at their great brain power, their handsomeness or beauty, or their power.

Understand that this powerful person has the ego of an eggshell. You do not want to be the recipient of the rage that erupts if you say something interpreted as a criticism. Stick strictly to work topics. Be extremely careful never to take away from the narcissist's self-image, judgment or success record.

Never suggest to the narcissist that they might have made a mistake. Remember the "I" not "you" discussion we had in Chapter 4 about relationships. The same applies here.

When you see missing figures from your narcissistic boss that need to be filled in, never say "You forgot to fill in this line of figures."

Instead, say "I believe I have made an error in finishing up this report on the sales statistics. I can't seem to locate the figures for the Denver office. Could you please help me?"

Many narcissistic bosses are bullies. They may swear and yell at you. In those circumstances, you need to maintain your own boundaries right from the beginning.

Remember the "I" and "You" rule. Never respond with your own anger and tell them "you can't speak to me like that."

Instead, calmly say "I am uncomfortable with being sworn at and yelled at." Then stop speaking. Allow time for the boss's mumbled "sorry." Instead, if they persist and unleash even more of a tirade you must find the courage to seek help from your human resources office. And keep standing your ground, even the second time, by saying calmly, "I am still uncomfortable with being sworn at and yelled at."

It takes great courage to take a complaint about a narcissist to a higher level, but if abuse is involved, you must do so. If twice you told your boss that you were uncomfortable with being sworn at and yelled at and they continued to berate and bully you, immediately go back to your computer and send an email to your boss.

In calm and professional tones, recount what happened and send it to the boss and send a copy to your home computer as well. Say something like:

"On two occasions on this date (cite date, time and year), I have expressed my discomfort to you for being sworn at and yelled at. Having just experienced it again, I am sending this memo pointing out once again that I feel uncomfortable being sworn at and yelled at."

That is sufficient. If it happens again, the next time add something like:

On three occasions since Monday (cite date, time and year) I have verbally expressed my discomfort at being sworn at and yelled at, and on one occasion (cite date, time and year) and again now (cite date, time and year) I am again expressing in writing my discomfort at being sworn at and yelled at.

This time send it to your boss's boss and/or your Human Resources manager.

If you accept the abuse, it will just continue to get worse. If you can set reasonable boundaries, you can survive.

Do not think if the narcissistic boss ultimately apologizes and changes their behavior that they are sorry they hurt your feelings or that they feel anything at all for how you feel. They don't and they won't. They are only offering up the apology now because they have been forced to for their own survival.

Your narcissistic boss cannot even imagine how you feel because they are incapable of having empathy. If forced by others to apologize to you, they may try to find other ways to be disagreeable to you. Continue to respond in a calm but firm manner and gradually, like any bully, they will turn to an easier target.

Studies have shown a strong link between narcissistic bosses and bullying. In fact, a 2007 study by scientists Catherine Mattice and Brian Spitzberg determined that narcissists were inclined to use bullying tactics. The study, done at San Diego State University, determined that the way narcissists preferred to bully was by excessively checking the work of their subordinates, spreading malicious gossip, withholding crucial information that would affect another person's work, ignoring co-workers, reminding people of their mistakes repeatedly, and ordering people to do work below their competency level (i.e. asking the computer programmer to take out the trash).

Narcissists preferred those subtle forms of bullying over more direct bullying tactics like shouting, threatening, making false claims against others and constantly criticizing their work.

What techniques can you use to tame the narcissistic boss?

First, you must understand that they are not going to change regardless of what you do. They need professional help. What you can do is protect yourself as well as possible. If the situation becomes unbearable, and the narcissist is firmly entrenched, you may have to seek alternate employment.

In the meantime, take a realistic assessment of the relationship between you and your narcissistic boss. Is it something you can deal with if you recognize the person for the mentally disturbed person they are? Can you stop expecting that they will appreciate you or respect you or even care about you at all? Can you keep your private life totally to yourself and do your best to support the narcissist and ensure that you do not contradict or criticize them?

Can you maintain your professionalism even in the face of unreasonable demands and the occasional rage from the narcissist?

Can you manage to flatter your boss a bit?

When your narcissistic boss moves too far into your professional boundaries, can you calmly and courageously stand your ground.

Can you document your accomplishments in case the narcissist unfairly turns on you in a rage and dismisses you unfairly? Can you keep good records to show what you are doing as well as memos from your boss that are disrespectful or suggest inappropriate actions to you or the company?

Are you willing to take the criticism when it is distributed and never retaliate? Will you pay attention to the many little things that the boss considers major annoyances and ensure that you avoid them?

Can you build a strong network of support both within the organization and outside of it?

It is ironic and the worst, but most narcissistic bosses sometimes rule over extremely effective teams. What is not always clear to the board of directors is that in the face of terror and unreasonableness, the workers sometimes band together to take care of each other and ensure loose ends are all tidied.

A discussion of the narcissist in the workplace would not be complete without a consideration of what happens if the narcissist is finally exposed for what they are and dismissed from their powerful post.

Immediately, the narcissist will conclude it was not his or her fault. They will rail at the people around them, at their spouse and children, at their families and anyone else who will listen. They will not assume any part of the responsibility for what happened.

A situation like a job loss can seriously unhinge a narcissist. Keep in mind that they have a grandiose image of themselves and an exaggerated sense of their own power and might. When the big pay checks stop and the humiliation of being unemployed hits, the results can be devastating.

The narcissist may have an entire psychotic episode. Extra security measures should be taken to protect those who have dismissed such an employee. Others may turn to extremely abusive behavior.

For the narcissist, however, the best reaction, and quite a few do this, is to retreat briefly to mourn and then return to re-establishing a grand identity again, assuming power where none exists, assuming accomplishments where none exist, and assuming superiority where none exists.

Some narcissists are so successful at rebuilding themselves that within months they are back at the helm of another corporation, claiming what happened in their former company was all a big misunderstanding on the part of a number of stupid board of directors.

Chapter 6: When you can't see the world as others see it

Most people have Facebook accounts, but did you know that a professional therapist could likely tell from viewing it whether or not you are a narcissist?

In a research project conducted at the University of Georgia, Laura Buffardi and W. Keith Campbell studied how the significant growth of social networking sites could yield clues to personality traits.

They selected Facebook in particular because it has more than 100 million users, a fertile ground for their study.

Clearly, not everyone who uses Facebook is a narcissist. But the researchers did discover that narcissists who use the site do it in a self-promoting kind of way that is identifiable to others.

By giving personality questionnaires to nearly 130 Facebook users, the scientists analysed the content of the pages and then had untrained people who had no connection to the subjects view the pages and determine where they felt the owners rated with regard to narcissism.

What was interesting was that while the trained therapists had no trouble picking out the narcissists, neither did the untrained people.

Some distinctive factors for the narcissist's Facebook site included having a much higher than normal number of friends, consistent with the narcissist's ability to attract a number of people but develop only shallow relationships with them.

Narcissists were also more apt to have glamorous pictures of themselves on the site, and very self-promoting pictures, unlike the snapshots non-narcissists use.

The study, which was published in the *Personality and Social Psychology Bulletin*, built on the work of earlier researchers who found that narcissists were more apt to have personal web pages than others.

It was just one more subtle indication that narcissists see the world somewhat differently than everyone else.

If you have established that you are a narcissist, this chapter will give you insight into how you see the world from a unique perspective. For those whose have narcissists in their lives, it will be a glimpse into a new perspective on your own world as seen through the eyes of someone who doesn't see what you see when they look at the same thing.

As we are learning, narcissism is a complicated disorder. The narcissist, while malfunctioning in many areas of their lives, is often extraordinarily effective at their work and driven to achieve tremendous things. Along the way they will alienate many people, but that is really of no consequence to them.

The biggest difference between the world of the narcissist and the non-narcissist is how other people are viewed.

If you are a narcissist, other people are basically inconsequential in your life. They are there to serve you and admire you. If they do anything other than that, they are annoying. Everyone around you is less intelligent than you are, and less accomplished. Not one of them could hold a candle to you, even on your worst day.

Other people are to be used to get you to where you want to go. They have no real value to you other than in the context of usefulness. When they cease to be useful, or when they impede you in any way, they must be eliminated from your inner circle.

These other people, who see value in everyone, have a lot of trouble understanding that you see value in no-one. In times of conflict, they will innocently appeal to your better nature, totally uncomprehending that what they see is your nature and it has only one other side, and that is the rage side and it is worse.

That is why it is so difficult to be true and lasting friends with you. In a normal friendship, people support each other. They see the finer things in each other, and they understand that there is an implied informal contract of loyalty, of "being there" for each other.

As a narcissist, you find such a concept laughable. They should be glad to serve you, and if they need you, that is not convenient. You will not be there.

If, as a narcissist, you have a disagreement with someone, they will often be shocked at the depth of your anger and disdain and try to appeal to your better nature. They will beg you to consider someone else who will be hurt by the decision, they will assume that despite your anger, somewhere within you is what they would call a "heart," a nature where goodness simmers and rises to the top on occasion.

Such an assumption is false with the narcissist. What lies beneath the disdain is contempt. What lies beneath the contempt is even more contempt and any appeal for sympathy or empathy or a change of "heart" is fuel for a rant and a rage.

In your narcissistic behavior, there is absolutely no conflict. You have only one decision to make, and that is to decide what is best for you and stick to it. All other choices stem from that. In that sense, your view of the world is relatively uncomplicated. Yours is the behavior of black and white, while the average person has doubts and second chances and many shades of grey to peer through.

As a narcissist you can be incredible cruel. You can turn against your long-suffering spouse, your own children, your parents, your neighbors and your friends and not lose a minute's sleep over it. While those on the other end of your rage mourn and cry and consider ways to reach you, you have no such thoughts. People who hurt you have no right to expect anything at all from you, let alone compassion or change.

As a narcissist, when people talk to you, you hear only the part of the conversation that relates to you. If they discuss other things, you drown them out with your thoughts about yourself.

People who discuss their own vacations might as well whisper, because no trip matters unless you are taking it. People buying new homes or having new babies are just lips moving with nothing registering unless they involve you in a meaningful role.

If as a narcissist you fight with someone because they are ignoring or annoying you, and then you return to your normal life, you are always surprised if that same person comes back at you with a sneak attack. You do not expect that. Once you are done with them, you expect that they will be done with you.

Narcissists lack what other people describe as a conscience, that niggling inner voice that warns you your behavior is wrong or what you are contemplating is bad. As a narcissist, you have no inner voice. You have only a developed pattern of thought that tells you if you steal or kill, you will be punished in the courts of law for it. And that is the only thing that keeps your behavior and your disdain and contempt for others in check at all.

As a narcissist you tell so many stories about yourself that many of them are contradictions, sometimes even within the same conversation. A narcissist can say they want a turkey dinner for supper, and when you ask if they want it stuffed with cranberry dressing, they can appear surprised and say they didn't want turkey at all, that they never said that.

If a non-narcissist says they are going to paint a picture, a few minutes later the narcissist may ask why they bought paint because they never do art anymore. When you argue with a narcissist that you just said you were going to paint, they will simply deny that they ever said that.

In times of stress, all of us forget things or may perform contradictory acts or make contradictory statements, but when that stress is eased, we are generally consistent in our claims and our nature.

Not so with the narcissist.

If you are a narcissist you will contradict yourself endlessly even under times of calmness and if caught, deny it and believe that you are right and your challenger is wrong.

You take what people say and interpret it in a way they can never anticipate. If you confess your love or admiration to a narcissist, instead of being pleased that you love them almost as much as they love themselves, they will diminish you and be nasty, taking power over you and threatening to walk out of your life if you don't fall completely under their power.

If you are a narcissist, you cannot understand the world of the non-narcissist where they willingly and openly praise others and appreciate their talents without being threatened by them. Non-narcissists will support an up-and-coming musician because they believe they have much to offer; they will purchase art from a student because they believe it to be good and they want to encourage the young person to continue on the path they have chosen.

As a narcissist, however, you compare yourself to everyone who comes in contact with you and you must always feel that you are better than they are. Why would you purchase the music of a person who clearly can't write songs and sing them as well as you could? Why would you buy scribbles on a piece of paper when you are obviously capable of producing much finer art?

The concept of encouraging someone is just ridiculous. You have no interest or even an understanding of what that means.

As a narcissist, you are not happy to attend such pastimes as concerts or art show openings because they are either a waste of your valuable time, or if you see something that you think just might be better than what you can do, you will fall into a deep depression.

The average person works hard to keep positive thoughts in a prime position within them. They want to be happy, to be calm and serene, to see the best in the world and to find the good in the people they meet.

The narcissist has a dark and negative view of life. They are constantly concerned that their needs and their superior position is unchallenged, they are agitated and stressed. They believe the world is a nasty place and that the people they meet are out to get them.

The non-narcissist also sees the world and many aspects of it as a learning environment. They believe that they start life as empty vessels and they spend their days filling up their minds and hearts with knowledge and wisdom. Endlessly curious, they accept that they will fail sometimes or forget things, or do things wrong.

When someone offers guidance in the form of positive criticism, they are often pleased that the person cared enough to get them back on the right track. They learn from their errors and from those who would guide them.

As a narcissist, you have an opposite view of the world. You are always primed for attack, always looking after your own survival. You want to be superior, successful, and powerful and you fantasize about that endlessly. Calmness and serenity are for the dead. You know the world is a rotten place and that you cannot trust the people in it.

You are extraordinarily competitive in a way that your non-narcissistic co-workers and friends cannot comprehend. Whatever you see becomes a contest within yourself, a bet that you could have done it better. Your drive is often relentless. You know you are superior and you have to prove it.

To ensure that everyone around you knows your superior status, you criticize everyone and everything. You could do better. What you see is ridiculous, how could anyone think it was good or even acceptable.

But when someone dares to criticize you, you are crushed. How dare they not recognize your brilliance, your perfection? You will either attack your critic or you will withdraw to a deep and dark place where you try to nurse your wounds and figure out how to hurt the person who hurt you.

A non-narcissist has a pretty accurate view of their place in the world. For most of us, it is a humble corner where we lead our lives gently, raising our families, watching stars flicker and beach fires burning, learn to play a musical instrument or bake wholesome bread. We are grateful for the sun shining on our faces, for the peace that fills our heart when we see our children sleeping like angels in their little beds, and we feel the touch of those we love. We work, and we strive to do our best, but we often are content not to be the person in charge.

A narcissist can never know such peace in their world. Their world is a fantasy of their own creation, a world in which they must have power and beauty and adoration. They are the army generals, the presidents, the CEOs, and the extraordinary artists and inventors.

As a narcissist, you often find it very difficult to know where your fantasy world ends and your real world begins. The lines blur and you do not understand why people you see on the bus don't realize you are somebody famous. You should not have to wait in a line, you are so gifted they should be pleased for you to be present at all.

Like the Greek god you are named after, you see your world in a reflection and you are beautiful and powerful and accomplished in it. It is easy for you to be in love with yourself and understandable that everyone else should be in love with you too.

Your grandiosity can impact everyone around you. If you are in a position where you hire others in a company, you will seek out and hire only those that remind you of yourself. If you are operating a garage or a bakery, you will teach your staff to do things exactly as you do, for that is the best way.

As a narcissistic parent, you may force your children to be just like you, and if they fail to accomplish that, you will tell them they have disappointed you and cast them away.

You may have religion in your life but not in the way the average person does. You are not there to humble yourself and beg forgiveness for your sins. You are not there to seek solace and support from an almighty deity who can help you through life's tragedies and crisis.

Instead, you are there because you are God's special messenger, His chosen one. You are there to be an example to other lesser mortals as to how a perfect person should be.

The one part of the world that gives average people great joy is closed to you as a narcissist. You do not have the ability to laugh, to genuinely find something funny and to lift your spirits with a good chuckle or loud belly-laugh.

You don't understand jokes or riddles. You listen to them, perplexed. Why is everyone laughing? What was funny about that? You can't tell jokes, because you can't remember the punch line, because it means nothing to you.

There is a reason for this. Because you lack empathy, you cannot grasp the context of humor, which is usually a mild put-down of ourselves or others. You cannot grasp irony or why one human condition is amusing and another is not.

You might become the master of the sarcastic put-down and cause others to guffaw, but save your money and don't buy tickets to a comedy club. You are the person who will want their money back because nobody said anything funny.

If as a narcissist you have developed a good career in sales or in the public spotlight, you may learn jokes and how to deliver them from your staff, and you manage to secure laughs under those circumstances, but you will never really understand why people react to them that way.

You will often appear younger than you are to the rest of the world, a testament to a mind that carried no other burdens than looking after yourself. You will also have a great deal of knowledge about your area of work if you applied yourself, but your general knowledge of culture and the world around you is often strangely limited. You were not interested in absorbing the facts that you heard, because they did not involve you and thus, you were not interested.

It is vital for the narcissist to stay young and good-looking, and they are willing to go to great ends to bring Mother Nature along to their side. As a narcissist, you will always see your face as younger and more beautiful than people of your age. You will also be the first in your group tempted to endure plastic surgery to face lifts to preserve your youth. Remember, that face coming out of the reflecting pool has to look its best.

If you are a narcissist, it is not easy for you to share. You believe you are entitled to take what is around you and you cannot understand the purpose that could be served to share it with others. Your tendency to exploit your world stretches to the people in it. You will shamelessly use them and discard them as they are useful to you.

A few narcissists have a tendency to buy extravagant things just to prove they can get them. It is not uncommon for the narcissist, seeking the fastest car, the biggest house, the most exquisite gardens, to spend themselves into bankruptcy. This is unusual, however. Most narcissists instead are very frugal to the point of being mean and miserly.

You will dress yourself in excellent clothes or knock-offs with the right labels since the people around you are too stupid to know the difference, but expect your spouse and children to be clothed in what they can secure from thrift shops and second-hand stores.

When holiday seasons come around, as a narcissist you are quite possibly the world's worst selector of appropriate gifts. Again, your lack of empathy and your cruelty for not satisfying people with what they want dominate. You may even make a show of asking a loved one what they want, and then determinedly not get it for them and instead substitute something they have never even discussed.

As a narcissist, if you are seeking to satisfy your sexual needs, you consider yourself a great catch. Many narcissists through the ages have kept diaries of their sexual conquests. Because many narcissists can be charming and flattering when you are first getting to know them, they are able to lure partners to their beds. It is only later when a real relationship is sought that their shallowness becomes apparent.

You as a narcissist are a bit of an expert on having a series of short-term relationships that yield sexual pleasure to you and require virtually no emotional investment. In your own mind, you are God's gift to your sexual partner. But if your sexual needs involve power, you can be a dangerous partner. You want what you want and you will have it. Your partner's discomfort is of no concern to you. As far as you are concerned, they are lucky to be with you.

As a narcissistic lover, you may make outrageous demands on your partner. Depending on their neediness and their own sense of self-worth, you may be able to use their vulnerability to your own advantage.

When a narcissist looks at his or her world, there are some roles that are more suitable than others. The perfect life would be to achieve stardom in any field, a place where the world places you on a pedestal and rushes to meet your every need.

Someone would be there to handle your appointments, drive your car, do your hair and makeup, dress you and cook your meals. It could be the perfect world.

But psychologists tell us that even such an idealized lifestyle would not make the narcissist happy. Deep down, your insecurities would bubble, just waiting to rise to the surface.

And ultimately, the true nature of your personality surfaces and the world falls out of love with you. When that happens, the crashing down of your world echoes across all the front pages and newscasts of the world, and there is only ruin.

And of course, it is not your fault.

One of the ways most narcissists provoke a public or private relationship crisis is through their natural antagonism and their suspicious, negative and aggressive responses to those close to them.

This total contempt the narcissist has for other people ultimately cracks their eggshell existence and destroys the world they had built up.

A 2014 study at the University of Georgia by Joanna Lamkin and her associates tested the true contempt of narcissistic personalities towards those in their so-called inner circle.

Students were first asked to rank themselves on their narcissistic tendencies. Those who scored highest were then pulled aside for the second part of the study, which asked them to rate how much they like the people in their personal social networks.

Those rating highest for narcissism replied that they did not like them at all. They treated those close to them with utter disdain. The study was called "An examination of the perceptions of social network characteristics associated with grandiose and vulnerable narcissism."

What is most tragic about these differing views of the world between the narcissist and the non-narcissist, is that the former have great difficulty changing. Their view of the world is distorted, but it is truly engrained.

If you are a narcissist, seeing the world as differently as you do, it will be extremely difficult for you to enjoy a normal, long-term relationship in a family setting. If you are not a narcissist, but involved with one, you must take steps now to preserve yourself and your own self-esteem.

On the plus side, when disaster strikes, you will not be devastated as others are. You will never doubt that you did the right thing, you will know anything bad that happens is never your fault, and you will never be burdened by guilt or remorse.

Life in its own way is simpler from the narcissist's view of the world. You will be confident, for the most part, that you can deal with any challenge in life, because you are superior to others. You will be less stressed, because you know how to do everything better than others around you.

You will sometimes proudly proclaim that you will not have a heart attack from stress, that instead, you give others heart attacks. That is a source of accomplishment for you.

If you are trying to understand the perspective of a narcissist on the world, it is difficult. Try to consider how you feel when you are singled out for praise at work for completing a project effectively, or when friends tell you how beautiful you look with your new haircut.

A little inner part of you is happy with that.

And your self-confidence grows with one success after another until even in your normal world, you have a sense that you might be a little smarter or a little more talented than some of the people you work with.

Now magnify those feelings about 500 percent. Imagine if every day in your mind you were being praised for extraordinary accomplishments. Imagine if the people around you were even dumber than you think they might be. Imagine if that new hair style makes you so fetching that people stop in their tracks to gaze at your attractiveness.

If you can imagine such a world, you are coming closer to seeing the world from the narcissist's perspective. That is a process you can achieve.

Then understand that the narcissist will never, under any terms, see the world from your perspective.

That is the long and short of it all, the sweet and the bitter and the promise and the end.

You may understand the narcissist's world, but you can never really be an important part of it. They won't let you close enough and deep down, they are incapable of really caring about you.

In the next chapter, we will delve further into the perspective of the narcissist toward the world and their total inability to sense regret or take responsibility for their actions when things go horribly wrong.

Chapter 7: When life means never having to say you're sorry

In earlier chapters, we have discussed the fact that the narcissist feels no guilt for their cruelty towards others. People in their lives are there to serve them, and they will strike out with emotional and verbal (and sometimes physical) abuse just to make themselves feel more powerful.

The true narcissist will never feel guilt about that.

But if you are a narcissist, you will feel shame.

That is because while guilt is about other people and your feeling of having treated them badly, which you are incapable of experiencing, shame is about the self, and you are all about the self.

As a narcissist, you can be submersed in feelings of shame that have only to do with yourself. You feel shame when you are unable to accomplish something.

The narcissistic football player, for example, may go into a deep and painful period of shame if they fumble the ball. This shame can overcome their personality, sinking them into a deep pit of despair. He feels damaged.

Keep in mind that they are not feeling shame because they let their team down. They are feeling shame because they are denied the adoration they so richly deserve.

The average person can feel shame and ultimately recover from it. The narcissist may drown in it.

Shame becomes a pervasive, all-encompassing pain. As a narcissist, you replay scenarios over and over again in your head, feeling the experience and its impact on you again and again. You imagine other scenarios, ones in which you triumph, but in the end, the picture comes back to you in your moment of shame.

Shame makes you feel worthless and it can drive you to addictive behaviors such as drinking and gambling. You are looking to get in control of yourself again.

The shame you feel as a narcissist is part of the more depressing side of your nature. It is often accompanied by worry. You worry about things that could happen to you, things that some people might do to you, and things that might go wrong at work.

You take your overblown worries into your real world, becoming even more distrusting against those you worry will undermine your efforts to assume your rightful position.

It doesn't matter that you have faced the challenge before and overcome it, you worry all over again. You have no memory of overcoming it, you just have constant worry.

Next to shame and worry, a pervasive character trait is playing the victim. Victims are all about self and the attention-seeking narcissist soon realizes that if they can't get sufficient attention by being a super-achiever, they may be able to attract it by being a victim.

Kind-hearted people turn to help the victim, and the "victim" narcissist in turns takes full advantage of their weakness and ultimately takes what solace they offer and then casts them aside as beneath contempt.

A clever narcissist does not feel guilt, but he or she does comprehend that if they appear to have nothing, others will feel guilt and step forward to help them.

The narcissist believes they are indeed a victim, that they have been treated badly. When people offer to help, they take it without a second thought, and continue to take to feed their sense of entitlement.

Their initial charm and hard-luck story pulls people closer, and the narcissist weaves them further into his web so they can be hopelessly manipulated.

When a colleague or a friend endures no end of suffering and pain, it is a wise idea to become leery. They may be using it as a crutch to take your sympathy or support, and get you close enough to take advantage of you for life.

Even when things are going well, you worry that they will end badly and this fills you with anxiety. You are at heart a pessimist; your glass is always half empty and you are warily watching those around you, sure that they will drain the rest of it.

When the worry becomes too intense, it borders on paranoia. You plot and plan and anticipate the way people will stand in your way and block you from achieving what is rightfully yours.

If you are not driven to be a super-achiever and are worried about people who envy you might attack you, you let the worry drive you down to a point of inertia. You worry so much and envision so much going wrong that you can scarcely do anything.

You would go out and take over the world, but there are too many stupid people who stand in your way. They would get you, make no mistake about it.

In our discussion about narcissistic traits so far, we may be giving the impression that narcissism covers only one specific set of behavior traits. But as we go further into their handling of shame and vulnerability, we begin to see there are differences depending on whether they feel vulnerable or invulnerable.

It is fair to generalize all narcissists by saying they are self-absorbed.

If you are a narcissist you ooze a sense of superiority, from your well-dressed exterior to your haughty body language. People use adjectives like "arrogant" and "entitled" and even "mean" to describe your behavior.

But both male and female narcissists fall into two categories when it comes to discussing their vulnerability.

Evelyn, a secretary, is a vulnerable narcissist. She prides herself on her excellent filing skills, on her ability to keep schedules and background papers up to date and her superior skills in picking up significant office gossip that she trades with her boss for his undying admiration and appreciation. She knows that she could do his job better than he does; the man can't even organize a cup of coffee and a trip to the dentist on the same day. He is absent minded and unfocused on important issues.

She is extremely arrogant to the rest of the staff since they are not near the inner sanctum of power. Behind her back they say she thinks she runs the company. They only flatter and fawn over her when they need things, and she seems susceptible to that.

She is married to Tom, a truck driver, and she is jealous of his independence and his ability to get away a lot. She is fearful that he will find love on the road and leave her and keeps close track of where he goes and when he is coming back. Sometimes she calls the office on days she knows he is traveling just to make sure he is where he has said he will be.

But Tom props up her ever-hungry ego and constantly reminds this rather plain-looking woman that she is beautiful and the smartest woman he has ever met. He says things like that in front of her family and friends.

When she complains about her stupid boss and challenged co-workers, he listens. When she says she might just quit, he agrees that she needs to be happy and they will make it work no matter what.

Most of Evelyn and Tom's friends think Evelyn is a spoiled princess and Tom is a saint, but Evelyn thinks they consider her brilliant and can't understand why she would have married a truck driver. She reminds him regularly that she could have married many other men and even her boss is in love with her.

If Tom ever sticks up for himself and corrects her about something, she flies into a rage and won't speak to him for days on end. He left her once but she took just enough sleeping pills to simulate a suicide and he won't do that again.

Malcolm, on the other hand, is an invulnerable narcissist with grandiose ideas. He is a lawyer who married Anne, a legal secretary. She is beautiful, stopped work after they married, and devotes her entire life to making him happy.

But he does nothing for her. He belittles her. Every day he reminds her that she isn't even worth the bullet it would take to kill her. He sleeps with other women and reminds her how they fall all over him. He takes no pains to hide his affairs, and says she should expect it, since she is unable any longer to please him sexually.

Sharon would like to make some money so she could run away now that the children are on their own. But he keeps reminding her that she could no more pick up the work she used to do than nothing, that the whole world of business has changed and she doesn't have the brains to change with it.

When she finally gets the courage to tell him she is leaving, he flies into a rage and beats her so badly he breaks her ribs and blackens her eye. He warns her that as a lawyer he will make sure she never gets a penny of his money and that he will tell the children she has been having affairs over the years and that's why he finally kicked her out.

He swears he will kill her if she mentions divorce again.

So what is the difference between the vulnerable and the invulnerable narcissist?

Neither is pleasant to live with. But the vulnerable narcissist has some sense that they need the other person to be with them, and they are less aggressive and more inclined to think they are the victim and the world is just out to get them.

The vulnerable narcissist makes a major show of being hurt and treated badly and they seem to care a little that their partner recognizes how the world treats them badly and stands against the unfairness with them.

However, as with all narcissists, if their partner ever points out that maybe the situation isn't the same as they see it, or even mildly criticizes their response to a boss, for example, they will strike out in rage and be extremely defensive.

The invulnerable narcissist is more confident. If they get even a glimmer of an idea that their partner does not see them as a totally superior being, they will turn on them in a rage as well.

They have no sensitivity and a total indifference to how their partners see them. They know if one partner leaves them, they can easily find a replacement and likely a better one. They have a number of affairs just to reaffirm their attractiveness and desirability.

Both the vulnerable and the invulnerable narcissist are extremely difficult to live with. Both demand control of the relationship and power over all in their household. Whatever happens will never be their fault and they will not be responsible for anything that goes wrong, ever.

Chapter 8: How narcissists can take bragging to a new dimension

Edward runs a small land survey company from a tiny office at the back of the local post office. He is the only employee and there is no office staff. He makes his appointments, conducts the survey, writes it up and files it, completes his own invoicing and does his own taxes.

But if you meet Edward at a social gathering, you genuinely believe that he is one of the top land developers in his city. He knows all the ins and outs of different land deals, he speaks with great authority, and he drops into the conversation his degree from Harvard University.

In his office hanging on the wall are fake certificates from awards he never received. It took him hours to put them all together and frame them, but they look great and impress all the idiot clients who seek his services.

His business card says "president" and his degree from Harvard is really a certificate from the local community college.

Edward tells people he pioneered a system of land registration that the state uses and that has now been adopted in Canada. He was recently at a seminar presenting a paper about it. In reality Edward has never left Iowa and never even secured a passport.

He tells people he is thinking of branching out in his business and is looking at franchising his approach into neighboring states. He speaks well, dresses richly, and his eyes sparkle and his approach is charming.

People who meet him are immediately impressed. He has never had any trouble getting jobs, even from the times when he was a youngster. He can't keep any of them because he always knows how to do the boss's job better and he makes that abundantly clear.

Edward, a narcissist, is an expert at bragging. He takes the tall tale of how great he is to a whole new dimension.

In his mind, he could easily be the next governor of his state and the White House and Oval Office looms right behind that.

When he takes a taxi, he is arrogant to the driver to show his importance. When he dines out, he is difficult with the waiter, demanding the best table, picking out any flaws and indicating he has the power to make or break the business.

Bragging is an ever-present characteristic of the narcissistic personality. The ability to present yourself as something more than you are is an instinct and you are good at it.

In fact, a new study conducted at the University of British Columbia shows that narcissists actually are favored in job interviews over quietly competent but more modest personalities.

The study, led by Professor Del Paulhus, a psychology professor at UBC, concluded that narcissists have an immediate advantage because they are able to easily boast about their own accomplishments, they make eye contact, and they are relaxed and confident.

Paulhus discovered that the narcissists are very comfortable at self-promoting and in the average job interview, you really do have to self-promote to succeed and get the job. The braggart in this case can out-maneuver the modest person, even though the latter may be better qualified and would do a better job in the long run.

The study, published in the *Journal of Applied Psychology,* involved 72 job applicants who were video-taped during their interview. Half of them were Asian, coming from a culture where modesty is encouraged.

Both expert human resources personnel and non-expert listeners had to determine which applicants they would prefer to hire for the job.

Afterwards, the applicants were tested for narcissistic qualities using a test known as the narcissistic personality inventory questionnaire.

The results were that the more modest applicants, including the Asian applicants, fared worse than the narcissist. There was little difference in whether men or women were placed in the "definitely hire" category. The only distinguishing fact was that they were able to brag more and they actually ended up being identified with narcissistic traits.

If the narcissists were challenged in the interview by someone with more knowledge than they had, rather than reining in their bragging, they actually intensified it.

Once on the job, as we have already discussed, the narcissist becomes even more of a braggart and holds their power by belittling others who appear to have knowledge or power of their own.

Narcissists are the ultimate networkers as well, deftly passing themselves off as "experts" even if they have just read a book on the subject being discussed.

Why do narcissists feel such an urge to brag and present themselves as more important than they are?

Dr. Linda Martinez-Lewi, author of *Freeing Yourself from the Narcissist in Your Life,* (2008) attributes such behavior to the narcissist's attempt to fill up their emotional emptiness that goes beyond a basic longing or sadness.

She writes that theirs is a severe wound, a savage pain so deep that it feels intolerable. The narcissist lacks the inner resources to sustain themselves. They cannot turn to others for affection or solace, because they do not trust them and have distain for them. Even the narcissist realizes that the people who admire them are really inconsequential in their lives.

A narcissist brags to blow up their ego and sooth their inner pain. In this way they can hide the darkness of the shadow inside of them from the prying eyes of the world.

With charm and superficiality and a few stories exaggerating their power, prestige and knowledge, they can carve out a place for themselves. Quite frequently, it actually works and they find themselves at the helm of large organizations or in positions of power in governments, universities or other institutions.

Sometimes they work their way to rock star status, buffing up their ego daily with 10 imagined awards and accolades for every actual one received. They daydream about their acceptance speeches for Academy Awards or global peace prizes. Every book they write will be a bestseller, every song they write will be a mega-hit and every deal they sign will make them millions.

No matter how successful they will become, the narcissist will continue to brag and make their accomplishments sound even bigger than they really are. At every step they can shore up their vanity and fuel their grandiosity.

When you meet a narcissist, you may at first be intrigued and drawn to them by their easy charm and confidence. It is only when you start to hear the contradictions or pick up a thread of something that doesn't ring true that you get a clue to their true character.

You never actually "converse" with a narcissist because that implies a give and take. There is no giving from the narcissist. The talk is all about them, what they did, and how they did it. If you try to share some of your own experiences to build a rapport, they will rapidly be bored and puzzled even at why you would share a story that doesn't involve them.

If they are sitting at a table with a number of people and control of the conversation is wrestled away from them, they will find an excuse to leave or grow distant and withdrawn.

The bragging and the lies serve one other purpose to the narcissist, besides feeding their ego. They are tools to help the narcissist manipulate and gain control of people and the situation around them.

It rarely occurs to the narcissist that they will be caught in a lie because they assume the people they are speaking with are too stupid to catch them. After all, they have the superior intellect.

After all, lies to anyone are symbols of disrespect. They are ways of telling the person listening that they haven't the intelligence to really grasp what is going on.

In many cases, the narcissist actually succeeds in getting away with their lies because they are adept at weaving back and forth between truth and fantasy. People latch onto the familiar truths they hear, and even if the lie is confusing, they give the speaker the benefit of the doubt.

For the non-narcissist, a conversation can be quite an innocent venture, a simple back-and-forth exchange of information and opinion. For the narcissist, it is a complicated exercise in manipulating, a game of knowing just what to reveal and when to keep control of the exercise and benefit from any possible advantage that may be offered.

If they decide to play the victim card, as some narcissists do adeptly, they will present a version of truth that draws people to them. But if they believe a lie will serve them better, it will fall out of their mouths as easily as air is expelled from their lungs.

It is a wonder they are not exhausted at the end of a networking event, but many narcissists are strangely excited after such exchanges. Their ego has been boosted, their esteem stroked and they are ready for the next round. They are, for the time being, important.

And as writer T.S. Eliot suggested, half the harm that is done in this world is because of people who want to feel important. While they may not mean to harm you, they don't care if they do or they may not even see it because they are so totally absorbed in thoughts about themselves.

That pretty much sums up the narcissist.

Chapter 9: The darkest side of narcissism

Like salt and pepper, the ebb and flow of tides and the ying and yang of life, there is a partnership in the narcissistic personality that is inevitable.

It is also dangerous.

It is the connection between narcissism and rage.

People who know narcissists well will often comment that they don't want to get on the wrong side of them. For workers with a narcissistic boss, such a move could mean demotion or firing. For spouses, it could mean verbal, emotional or physical abuse. For friends it could mean spitefulness and vindictiveness at a level they couldn't even imagine.

The darkest side of the narcissistic personality is its short fuse. They are capable of blowing up at any time with the slightest provocation.

If you are a narcissist, you are likely described as a control freak, argumentative, a poor loser and a person who can't take "no" for an answer.

If your interests are not accommodated, you display an unreasonable level of anger. If you feel contradicted, criticized or humiliated, you will respond with rage. You will be boastful when you win, and sullen and angry when you lose.

It is difficult to explain the narcissist's capacity for rage. One way to demonstrate it is to consider different perspectives.

As children we were all taken at some point to a circus or a museum that had a variety of mirrors. One would show us an honest reflection of ourselves, but another would show us tall and thin and another short and fat.

We had enough self-awareness to understand which mirror was the true reflection and which one showed us with a distorted image.

The narcissist, however, operates without such a filter.

If you are a narcissist, you see the world through a mirror where everyone you meet admires you, flatters you, is envious of you and obeys you without question. When you look in a different mirror, you still see yourself as the person to be admired, flattered, envied and obeyed. You have no other filter that distinguishes your real image from your imagined image.

Therefore, if other people do not see what you see, if they fail to admire, to flatter, to envy and to obey, you feel like they are threatening you. When someone assaults you, you have no choice but to fight back and fight back you will.

You will fight back fiercer and harder and better than your attacker. You will rage and roar and you will win their submission.

In the narcissist's mirror, they are always larger than life. They are always bigger than anyone around them, they are always smarter, they are always more successful. They need to know that and be constantly reassured of it to stay stable in their world.

When you contradict a narcissist, it moves well past a simple disagreement.

Your words are a direct attack on their very essence. They must fight to preserve their self. Each fight, no matter how insignificant the issue, is a fight for survival.

As a narcissist, you must stop your attacker cold at the first assault, because should you allow them to land even one more blow, they could shatter you and you might never recover.

You are the tiger in the cage, cornered and wounded, ready to fight to the death. You will take no prisoners. You will have total compliance; compromises are for the weak and stupid.

Do not continue to fight with words once the narcissist flies into a rage. This is a battle you cannot win at this stage. Stay quiet and calm and let them rage to a standstill. Be careful not to provoke the fight further to a physical altercation because the narcissist at this point has lost all touch with reality and may harm you.

Some narcissists support groups suggest that a few hours after such a rage, you calmly tell the narcissist that you will simply walk away should that happen again.

The problem with that advice is that it can sometimes trigger yet another rage, fiercer than the first. If the narcissist is your spouse and you are not as powerful as they are, and if you are alone, you may instead wish to spend the next few hours contemplating your plan for leaving.

Most therapists do advise leaving the narcissists if it is at all possible. If it is not, they recommend getting professional help to learn how you can deal with a narcissist and better protect yourself from the inevitable rages.

If the raging narcissist is your boss, you may seek assistance from your human resources department, but if your company is small and you have no recourse, you may wish to spend the next few hours bringing your resume up to date and trolling for a different job.

It sounds defeatist perhaps, but it is rare that the narcissist will change. In many cases, when rage is involved, they will actually get worse. Any challenge will just evoke a stronger reaction the next time around.

Some narcissists do not rage when criticized but do not be lulled into thinking they are handling it well. These are the most devious narcissists of all. They will instead stay calm, but from that point forward they will plot actions and methods of getting their revenge on you.

When they are finished with you, you may well have preferred the rage.

If the narcissist is your spouse and their rage is limited to emotional and verbal abuse, not physical abuse, you may believe that you are strong enough to withstand it and ignore it.

Rarely will you be able to do that over a long period of time. A steady diet of belittling can destroy the self-worth of even the strongest person. Someday, when you are a little weakened because of some other circumstances in your life, the verbal rage will assail you and afterwards, you will start to wonder if you really are stupid or ugly or unable to stand on your own in this world.

From there it is a downward spiral to the point where the narcissist has complete control over you. That will not make them happy. They will seek ways to make you feel even worse, even more dependent on them.

That is no way to go through life. Narcissists can learn to automatically respond differently to certain situations, but rarely can their personality disorders be completely eradicated.

You have to know that there is a life after living with a narcissist and you deserve to find it.

A number of onsite groups now offer support to people whose lives have been impacted by relationships with a narcissist.

Some of these include Adult Children of Narcissistic Parents, Narcissist Abuse Recovery and Narcissistic Personality Disorder Forum.

Narcissism has a dark side and its impact on children, spouses, employees, other family members and entire communities can be devastating. There is no easy answer to dealing with a narcissist with uncontrolled rages, but they are inevitable and they rarely subside even with age.

Chapter 10: How narcissists use others to achieve their own ends

Narcissists are natural experts when it comes to controlling the behavior of the people and either charming or bullying them into supporting their own ends.

Despite their lack of empathy for others, they have an instinctive understanding of other people's weaknesses. Any clue they can gather, whether it is a detail about a co-worker's personal life or a vulnerability in a family member, can be exploited to gain psychological control over that person.

The narcissist has no qualms whatsoever about using people and then casting them aside when they are no longer useful. They are ruthless and uncaring when it comes to the concerns of others and the impact their actions have on others.

In some ways, that makes them natural leaders. Their ability to charm people helps them achieve political power; their ability to bully people helps them achieve corporate power. People work to support their grandiose image either voluntarily or begrudgingly, but the end result is the same and the narcissist doesn't care. Whatever works is his or her only concern.

How does a narcissist manage to manipulate people so successfully?

Harriet Braiker, a clinical psychologist and author of the book *Who's Pulling Your Strings? How to Break the Cycle of Manipulation,* (2004), identifies five common ways most people can be manipulated.

The narcissist is adept at all of them.

They include positive reinforcement, negative reinforcement, intermittent reinforcement, punishment and traumatic one-trial learning.

If you are a narcissist, you use positive reinforcement with your easy charm, flattery, smiles and praise. You will even use crocodile tears and then express outlandish gratitude for the efforts the manipulated person will take to solve your problem.

You will give little or lavish gifts, depending on how much effort you want from the person you are using. You will publicly recognize the person whose support you seek. You will apologize effortlessly if it will help you reach your end, give money and attention to the object of your manipulation.

The word "object" is used intentionally because for the narcissist, that is what people are. You do not see them as something akin to yourself; instead they are pawns in your masterful chess game and you need to line them up in the right position, using flattery or gifts or any other trick, to ensure that they win the prize.

Negative reinforcement is another useful manipulation technique. In it, you promise a person to remove something they do not want if they will do something they do not want to do.

In an office, it works like this.

"You will not have to come in and work Saturday morning if you take this home and finish this project tonight."

In reality, the person doesn't want to do either of the two choices, but they would definitely rather work Thursday night than Saturday morning when they have planned something with their children.

The narcissist is especially clever in using negative manipulation. If you share any personal information with them, they will remember and use it against you. In this example, the worker may have innocently let slip that they are planning to drive their son to a hockey tournament in a neighboring city on Saturday morning.

As a narcissist, you know this information and it is tucked into your excellent memory bank for use as needed. You know instantly that you can make this person work every night of the week if necessary, just so they will be free to do what is obviously important to them on Saturday morning.

Intermittent or partial reinforcement is often enacted with the vague promise of something better to come down the road, sweetened with just enough evidence to make it look real, even though the narcissist has no intention of letting the promised event happen.

Again, in an office setting, the narcissist will ascertain who is ambitious and play on that. He or she will promise that person that if they step up to the plate and complete a mega-project on their already full schedule, they will do their best to get them a spot in the head office's golf tournament next month.

The promise is purposefully vague. You might even say: "Now I can't guarantee this, but I will do my best to see if I can get you included in the head office golf tournament next month."

The ambitious person is willing to dive in in the hopes that they can swim with the top dogs. When the golf tournament happens, his opportunity does not materialize of course, but the narcissist will already have a perfectly valid excuse.

Punishment as a method of manipulation involves the trademark narcissistic behavior of rages, bullying, intimidation, threats, sulking, laying on the guilt, emotionally blackmailing and even playing the victim.

Narcissistic parents often use these techniques on their families but will bring them into the office as well and often get away with it.

They will holler at people, demand results, nag for completion of projects in impossibly short times and swear and carry on. People will run for cover, and work as fast as they can to complete the project and feed the raging beast.

Traumatic one-trial learning usually involves one specific incident that is so awful for the recipient that they succumb to the control of the narcissist and spend their time trying to appease them.

Usually in an office this involves rage from the narcissist, threats of losing a job, threats to expose a failure of the worker to a higher office and threats to create a permanent black mark on their record.

The person receiving the threats believe them to be true and is so overwhelmed with the potential of them being carried out that they will go to any lengths in the future to avoid upsetting the manipulator.

Dr. George Simon, a leading world expert on manipulators and disturbed people, provided more insight into the manipulative mind in his 1996 international bestseller *In Sheep's Clothing: Understanding and Dealing with Manipulative People.*

Dr. Simon, who has a degree in clinical psychology from Texas Technical University, believes that manipulators gain their power by their ability to exploit vulnerabilities in others.

They especially target the naïve who cannot believe somebody can just be devious and ruthless with no good intentions whatsoever, the over-conscientious person who believes everyone should be given the benefit of the doubt, and the person with low self-confidence who lacks the assertiveness to say no even to outrageous demands.

Manipulators also seek out the person Dr. Simon calls "over-intellectualized" meaning they try too hard to understand the manipulator, believing they have some valid reason for being so hurtful. Emotionally dependent people with submissive personalities are also magnets for manipulators. Both the over-intellectualized and the submissive are easy pickings for the narcissist.

But a narcissist, while preying on the vulnerable, will tackle anyone and find a way to manipulate them. Confident in their own superiority, they believe they can get the best of anyone.

Once the narcissist achieves what they want from the person they are manipulating and they are no longer useful, they discard them. It does not matter if the person has been their friend for 20 years, their neighbor for 10 years, or their colleague who has steadfastly been loyal to them and helped them build their career. In a narcissist's world, everyone is expendable. There are plenty more where they came from.

If you are a narcissist, you will also manipulate people by lying or by withholding information.

If the person being taken advantage of rears up in anger and threatens to make trouble, the narcissist immediately denies they have done anything wrong. They can be very effective in their denial, because they believe it. The narcissist never does anything wrong in their own eyes.

If the denial is not believed, the narcissist will rationalize their abhorrent behavior. They will have an excuse, and it will be a good one. Or they will minimalize the incident. They will acknowledge that the behavior occurred, but that it is not nearly as harmful or bad as the other person is suggesting. If they are accused of saying something inappropriate, for example, they will swear that it was just a joke and was never intended to be hurtful.

If the person who has been taken advantage of confronts the narcissist alone, they may simply ignore them. A standard response is to raise up a hand and indicate "I am too busy to discuss this now," or "I'm not going to credit that with a response," or words to that effect.

If pressed to pay attention, they may listen briefly and respond by totally diverting the conversation in another direction. In such an instance, the new topic may be critical of the behavior of the complainant in some other area of their life. The message, however, is clear. What they are suggesting is that if you want to press this complaint against me, I have lots of fire power to light back in your direction.

Close to this, but a slightly different tactic, is for the narcissist to shame the complaining person and raise their self-doubt about whether the manipulation really occurred as they remember it. The idea on the narcissist's part is to embarrass the complaining person, to make them feel that they never should have challenged them at all.

Narcissists, when confronted with claims that they have used people, will often evade the issue or intimidate the person who challenges them. In some cases, especially with family members, the narcissist will lay a guilt trip on the complainer, telling them they have life much easier than the narcissist does and that they can't believe they would trouble them over such a trivial manner.

Sometimes the narcissist will play the victim or vilify the real victim. This is common in cases of sexual abuse or even inappropriate sexual remarks in the workplace. The narcissist will insist that the victim came onto them and when rejected, accused them of touching them or saying something inappropriate. The "he said/she said" scenario can be very difficult for corporations to discern.

Ever the master manipulators, the narcissist may even pretend to be shocked or confused at allegations of bad behavior. Their goal is to make the complainant doubt themselves and it often works.

Knowing that narcissists manipulate people and that they respond badly when challenged for their manipulating habits, we must still consider the question: what is it in the narcissist's make-up that makes them need to manipulate people. After all, they consider themselves superior and gifted. Why push other people to do things they aren't inclined to do naturally?

If you are a narcissist, chances are the number one reason you manipulate people is simply to advance your own agenda. You want to achieve your goals and gain power, wealth and honors. Often you need other people to help you get there and manipulating them is the easiest way to build your army of helpers.

You may also manipulate just to experience the feeling of power that accompanies getting someone else to serve you. Feeling in control fills a deep need within you. Your own self-esteem is glorified and made stronger by the more people you have power over.

Because of your disregard for other people, you may also manipulate them out of boredom, just as a game and a way of hurting them. You have contempt for them anyhow. Why not see what you can make them do? In your world, it may be more fun than watching television or going out to lunch.

Chapter 11: Why we all need a healthy dose of narcissism

Most of us have what we describe as good days and bad.

Some mornings we wake up and we feel ready to take on whatever challenges come our way. We dress for the day and our reflection from the mirror says "you look good," and our mind tells us "you are on your game today."

Other days, we feel the weight of the world on our shoulders. The reflection in the mirror says "you look tired today and aren't those new wrinkles around your eyes?" Our mind tells us "you can do this as long as one more thing doesn't come crashing down around you."

Everyone's self-esteem swings like a pendulum between good days and bad, but normally the radius of the swing is well within normal limits.

For people with perennially low self-esteem however, the radius of the swing in the bad direction goes further and further until it threatens to swing into oblivion and they feel they will drown in despair.

Some signs that your self-esteem is getting dangerously low is when all you recognize in yourself are your limitations and weaknesses and faults. You cannot credit yourself with solving anything, with figuring out life or the challenges it throws at you. You place no value on what you think and wait to hear what others think before you can decide what to do about anything. Everyone around you, in your eyes, is smarter and more accomplished than you are.

In your eyes you are a failure and likely always will be. Success is for other people to enjoy, not you. Even when someone praises you for work well done or how nice you look, you don't believe them. You can't accept nice things being said about you.

Your conviction that you will fail at whatever you try keeps you from trying things that you could actually do. It is a sorry cycle and unfair to you and the person you could be if your self-esteem could swing back and forth in a healthier radius.

On the other end is the growing high self-esteem. Every day your pendulum of emotion swings a little farther to the belief that you are great and successful and better than those around you. Gradually and over a period of time, your high self-esteem swings higher and higher and higher, right off the scale and one morning you wake up to feel so highly about yourself that you have become a narcissist.

At a more reasonable level, of course, a high self-esteem is generally good for you. It means you have more self-knowledge, that you recognize that you have some talents and skills and the ability to use them. Your view of yourself is more accurate than the person who feels everything they touch will be a failure.

When you have a healthy self-esteem, it is not that you believe you are perfect; it is just that you recognize your flaws but believe you have more good qualities than bad ones. You have a balanced personality.

In a balanced personality, you have the confidence to meet life's challenges face to face. You believe you have the capability to deal with life and work and raising a family and all the dimensions that create a full life. You may have moments of doubt, but overall, you function effectively in a busy world.

You have, in essence, a touch of narcissism, but yours is a healthy sense of self that will spur you to take a few risks, achieve some substantial successes, and relate well with people and build genuine, lasting relationships that will support you through your life.

How do you know when your healthy self-esteem is swinging past the radius into unhealthy or overly narcissistic?

When you begin exaggerating your importance and boasting about your accomplishments, you are moving into the danger zone. If that is coupled by your feeling that you are superior to everyone around you, then you are becoming a narcissist.

Gradually you start to feel contempt for those around you. You imagine that you are the only one who really understands what is going on and how to do things properly. You believe you are more gifted and skilled than everyone else.

What you are experiencing is not just a healthy self-confidence but an unnatural love for yourself that covers your hidden insecurities.

The struggle between low and high self-esteem is part of human nature and none of us are immune to it.

To have a healthy self-esteem means you are able to live a full and purposeful life, to develop lasting relationships and to look upon the world as a good place to be. You are open and curious about things, and constantly learning.

You are not afraid to express what you think or what you need. You make decisions easily and you are comfortable with them. You don't have to consult everyone else and beg them to make your decisions for you.

You build great relationships. If for some reason you get hooked up with a friend or partner who does not respect you or is emotionally, verbally or physically abusive, you leave. You know your own worth and are not willing to be a victim to anyone.

You have a pretty good idea about what you are good at and what you can do with the skills and talents you are given. You also know what you are not skilled at, and you do not attempt the impossible. People describe you as having "common sense."

If something bad happens in your life, you possess the ability to bounce back. You may be crushed or hurt or grieving, but over time, the force of your confidence returns and you are able to resume a full life.

At the same time as you fill up your own life with your work and relationships, you are usually respectful of others. You are not constantly criticizing the people around you. You see people who accomplish wonderful things and you acknowledge that. You do not always believe that you could do better.

Because you see reasonable worth in yourself, you are confident enough to see worth in others. You can give praise and take criticism.

You are not inclined to be consumed with guilt or shame because as a general rule, you behave in a civilized fashion and treat people decently. You are able to forgive yourself if you make a mistake and just as importantly, you have the capacity to forgive others.

You are less likely to develop an addictive habit and less likely to become anorexic or succumb to some other eating disorder.

As you go through life with a healthy dose of self-esteem, you are happier, more optimistic and more selfless than people with low self-esteem. You are also living a fuller and more balanced life than the narcissist.

Being assured of your self-worth to a healthy degree means being able to accept responsibility for the way you live your life and for your deeds and thoughts.

Furthermore, at every stage of life having a healthy dose of narcissism is considered a good thing. For example, children who see value in themselves have more balanced personalities. They believe that they are worthy of love and strong friendships, while at the same time they are open to growth and aware that they can develop further.

They are willing to offer others their skills and positive attitude to the world and they are comfortable amid their family and friends. They are able to accept a reasonable share of food, love, resources and attention from their place in the family.

They are natural problem solvers, and that skill spreads over into their relationships. They are willing to work to get through conflict with others and to stand by their friends and siblings during rough patches.

They are more likely to tell someone they trust if they sustain abuse.

They are also willing and able to tackle new challenges, to learn new things and to explore the world with an open and curious mind.

The same cannot be said for children without healthy narcissism. Their lives are not nearly as positive.

Children who have low self-esteem are more likely to feel sad, guilty, angry and ashamed of themselves. They do not believe they really deserve good things if they come their way.

Their behavior is more negative and they do not perform as well at school. Convinced they are not smart and cannot do as well as their smarter colleagues, they will indulge in self-defeating behavior. They work themselves up to a high state of anxiety prior to a test, for example, and are unable to perform to their best, even though they may actually have the correct answers. Their boding sense of failure thus becomes a fact.

When they do fail, it is almost as if they are telling themselves, "I told you so." It confirms their negative thoughts about themselves and sends them spiraling still further down the tunnel that ends in negativity and self-fulfilling failure predictions for the future.

Parents have an important job to help their children nurture an inner sense of self-worth and a healthy dose of narcissism to help them have a happier, more fulfilling life.

No matter what they do or what others do, a child must know inside that they are a person of value. We must teach them to be confident in their own worth and not gauge from a comparison to somebody else. In fact, children need to understand that they are valuable in this world and it has nothing to do with how they relate to other people. We must explain to them that no matter how gifted they are, or how beautiful, or how accomplished, there is always someone else who surpasses them in some area.

A study conducted at the University of Michigan's Institute for Social Research showed that basing our own self-worth on comparisons and opinions of others is really detrimental at any age.

The December, 2002 study, headed by psychologist Dr. Jennifer Crocker and published in *Journal of Social Issues,* determined that college students who based their sense of inner value on external sources, such as the favorable opinion of others or higher academic test scores than others, had more stress, conflict with relationships, more anger and academic programs, and increased levels of drug and alcohol use and eating disorders than those who were comfortable that they were worthy on their own.

It is interesting what yardsticks the college students used when measuring their own self-worth against factors outside of themselves. Eighty percent of them used their academic marks and overall success, 77 percent used family support, 66 percent said they just needed to be doing better than others and between 65 and 70 percent of the female students said they based their self-worth on their appearance.

What you measure yourself against, the study showed, did not necessarily motivate you to perform best competitively. For example, the students who based their self-worth on their high academic scores actually did not receive higher grades overall. They did study more each week and were highly motivated to succeed, but they really did not achieve any more success than students whose self-esteem was not tied to their marks. However, the students who did measure their worth against their academic scores were more stressed and reported more conflicts with their professors.

Crocker concluded that when a student measures their self-worth against their academic averages, they may be full of anxiety and fear of failure and that stress load could be interfering with their memory when they are writing examinations.

Students who believed themselves to be good people, virtuous and moral, did receive high grades and had fewer issues with alcohol, drugs and eating disorders.

As a result of the study, Crocker urged people to focus their goals on something larger than themselves. People who could think bigger thoughts than themselves, such as how their actions could contribute to others, were more inclined to have a healthy dose of self-esteem and be freed from negative thinking.

When you are helping your children (and yourself) to develop just enough narcissism to get by in life, it helps to consider all the uniqueness that creates you as an individuals. We have sets of talents and skills that make us unique and give us unique value. Rather than rating ourselves on the scale of self-esteem, we need to create a climate in which we can just be ourselves.

What do you do if your narcissism is lacking? How can you fill yourself up with just enough self-esteem, but not swing your pendulum too far into completely self-serving behavior?

Here are seven steps towards building a health sense of narcissism so that you can better lead a richer, fuller life:

1. Stop measuring your worth against other people's. In science classes as children, we

are taught the folly of trying to compare apples and oranges. While the two fruits may be similar, they have different nutritional components, they have different tastes and appearances, and each one gives value to our bodies in their own way. However, as adults, we believe that we can compare ourselves to our neighbor, to our co-worker or even to a sibling and that it is a fair comparison. It is not. There is nothing to be gained using others as a system of our own measurement. We have value, regardless of what anybody else does. If we lived on a desert island and there was nobody around us, we would still have value.

2. Silence your inner critic. The lower our self-esteem is, the louder our inner critic speaks to us. It reminds us we are overweight and plain-looking. It tells us we are slow to grasp new concepts and that we will never be successful. It is a cruel voice and it has no business lurking inside of us. It has been a freeloader in our heads since childhood and it is time to move it out and make space for new thoughts. The inner voice is the voice of people who have been unkind to us in the past. It is the voice of our self-doubt. It is the voice that keeps us from being all that we can be. Take it in stages. Turn it down. Then make it whisper, and finally,

summon the courage and just turn it right off!

3. Be kind to yourself. We have all heard of the movement "Random Acts of Kindness" where strangers help each other by doing something generous of spirit to lighten the load of another. But how many of us ever practice a random act of kindness on ourselves? Perhaps we could start small. How about allowing ourselves a 15-minute break every afternoon where we sip tea or coffee and read one chapter from an uplifting book? Can we progress to getting a professional hair style? How about the gift of a walk around our block in the sunshine? Can you pick some fresh wildflowers and place them on your kitchen table to lift your spirits for several days. Just for a few minutes every day, be kind to yourself. Then try to grow that time into a day off, a holiday or an exciting adventure that you have always wanted to do. You deserve some gentleness and kindness in your life and there is no reason it can't come from you.

4. Respond to your own suffering. There is a huge difference between wallowing in self-pity and respectfully responding to your own suffering. It is pointless to pretend you are fine when something horrible happens such as losing the love of

your life or someone you care about. You cannot just submerge bad things in your mind and shovel a little more work on top of them and think they will go away. You have to respect the fact that you have been hurt, accept it as a hurt, and develop a strategy to deal with that hurt and move on. Psychologists call it the art of self-compassion. When you acknowledge your suffering and you respond to it, you can gentle move it from an ever-present hurt to a new place of memory. Over time that hurt just becomes a part of your colorful life experience and its hold on you diminishes.

5. Acknowledge that your imperfections are lovable. Have you ever gone to the animal rescue shelter to get a puppy and selected the ugliest little dog in the litter? There is something in colossal ugliness that ends up being cute. That is a good thing to keep in mind when you worry about your own imperfections. What we consider to be a horrible part of our makeup can end up being charming and endearing to others; it is all about perspective. We are all imperfect in some way and that is the bond that draws us all together as human beings. Accept your imperfections as part of the mystery of life and do not let your thoughts be dominated by them. Most people won't even notice them and those who love you will love them as part of you.

6. Add meaning to your life. In building a healthy dose of narcissism, we are focused on our sense of self. But it is also important to move past the "self" and look out on the world and see how you can get involved in participating in activities that bring meaning to your life. Doing work that matters is a soothing balm to all that hurts you. When you lose yourself in a cause bigger than yourself, at the end of the day you feel better, even though you are not sure how it happened. Being generous and connected to good deeds is good for your self-esteem. It will make you feel better, simple as that. Positive energy breeds positive energy.

7. Develop principles you believe in and are comfortable with and stick with them. Having a set of values, it turns out, helps you place value on yourself. When you make an effort to match your actions to what you believe in, your feeling of self-value increases. Problems arise when you act differently from what you think you should actually be doing.

Besides building a better life for yourself with a high self-esteem, you will also be viewed differently by others. People who exhibit low self-esteem either by always appearing the victim or being overly proud of themselves to the point of arrogance repel people. But confidence and an enthusiasm for life is attractive and brings people towards you.

Loving yourself is not an extreme love affair that we have been discussing on the far end of narcissism. Rather, it is understanding that you have value in your world and deserve to live life productively and happily. It means being at peace when you are by yourself and joyful when other people arrive to share your experiences with you.

It is not an act you can put on for the evening. People will see right through you if you aren't genuinely okay with the way you are. Loneliness and neediness have ways of bubbling to the surface even while you are steering the conversation in another direction.

If you try all the ways we have presented to build your self-esteem and you still feel unworthy of the life you want to lead, try to figure out when you feel your self-esteem at the lowest. Is it at work with a bullying boss? At home with a difficult spouse or children who constantly challenge your right to parent? Is it when you are with your family or your friends?

By identifying the kinds of situations that shake your self-worth to the core, you can take action to protect yourself. In some cases it will be as simple as breaking the tie between you and someone who wants to spend time with you but is very negative about everything. In other cases it may mean changing jobs or leaving a relationship. None of those solutions are easy, but they are essential if you are going to be the person you deserve to be.

Self-esteem can also be shaken when dramatic changes occur in our lives, such as divorce or the death of a spouse, the loss of a job you have held for a long time, or even a child moving away from home. Some people, after happy and productive lives, lose their self-esteem when they retire. Their identity was wrapped up in what they did, not in who they were, and when the work routine evaporates, so does their self-esteem.

Knowing what is triggering the feelings about your self-worth is a good first step to addressing them. Now try to analyze what happens to you when you are in the company of those people that upset your value of yourself and if there is something you can do to protect yourself. Are you interpreting the situation correctly? Are your reactions to what is happening rational or irrational?

Can you step back from the situation and study it with less emotion to try to figure out a solution?

Oftentimes, a good conversation with ourselves is all we need to change the way other people manipulate us. Sometimes we were being worked to another person's needs without our knowledge. We were reacting instinctively to what appeared to be one situation, when in fact the manipulator was working us to that conclusion through a clever set of lead-up steps.

Once you figure out if your reaction is based on what is really happening, or if your emotions and perceptions, played on by another, are leading you to false conclusions, you will be better able to confront the situation directly.

Other than false perceptions, there are number of other ways of thinking that can threaten your sense of self-worth and cause you to feel bad about yourself without any logical cause. Quite often they are situations you find yourself in because of a certain way of thinking, and that thinking can easily be changed.

For example, suppose you are upset with a neighbor. It doesn't even matter what started it; what matters now is that you want total capitulation on his or her part or you are ready to pursue the disagreement all the way to the court level. You are angry and agitated all the time; your home is no longer the pleasant place you used to love because at the very sight of it, all you can think of is your anger with your neighbor.

You have laid down terms in the agreement, and for you, it's all of nothing. He is ignoring you and this is hurting your self-esteem still further. You are wondering if you have any value because this person will not do what you want.

If you step outside of yourself for a few minutes and look at the situation from a different perspective, you may discover that you would actually be happy with one action on his part. You do not have to indulge in all or nothing bargaining. A compromise where you drop some of your grievances and he agrees to address the others might work perfectly well.

All-or-nothing thinking also erodes your esteem when you place your entire self-worth on the line to reach an impossibly high goal. You might say "if I don't make 100 percent on this test, I am not worthy of being in this course." Nobody else is expecting to make a perfect mark, but because you have set that goal and determined that it is an all-or-nothing moment in your life, not reaching that goal will seriously damage your self-esteem.

Dwelling on the negative things in life is another self-esteem attack. Some little thing goes wrong on your way to achieving a goal, and you let it totally derail you. You believe that if you missed one step on the way to the journey's end, you can never reach your destination. You believe everyone is watching you and they have seen you fail and will never believe in you again. This destructive thinking can push you out of the realm of healthy narcissism and into a danger zone.

Try to reconsider just how important the step you missed was, and if there isn't some other way you can resurrect the challenge and move on.

Still on the subject of negative thinking, if you find yourself constantly turning good thoughts and actions into bad, you are also in danger of damaging your self-esteem. People give you a genuine compliment, for example, and you dismiss it because you believe they want something from you. You do well on a project, and instead of enjoying the moment before moving on to the next challenge, you chide yourself that you only did well because it was easy. You are uncomfortable with being told you did a good job; you are damaging your self-esteem.

When building up your self-esteem always remember that just because you think a thought or have a feeling, that does not make it real. At its extreme, you may say you feel like a failure, but that does not mean you are one. You may feel that the boss is singling you out for particularly harsh treatment, but perhaps the boss is being tough on everyone.

When people don't do the things you expect, do not immediately assume that it is because they don't value you and thus, you are not worthy of value. Things happen in other people's lives that don't mean anything to you, but are extremely upsetting to theirs. A parent who is up all night with a sick child and really needs to be home early today to get them to a doctor may refuse your offer for coffee. You are devastated. Clearly they place no value on your friendship. You are leaping to the wrong conclusion. The person is all wrapped up in their own crisis of the moment and will call you another day when things calm down.

To stay within the healthy radius of the esteem pendulum swinging back and forth between positive and negative, be sure to avoid overreacting to any situation. When you can find a calmness and patience within yourself, you start to realize that you have value, but that the entire world doesn't revolve around your particular life.

Speak in hopeful terms. In times of trouble, it is okay to acknowledge to yourself and others that you have hit a rough patch, but don't end there. Phrase your story in hopeful terms. Say things like "yes, it is true that I have received a difficult diagnosis, but I have done a lot of research and the prognosis is good."

Understand that sometimes you just won't measure up to your own standards. You will make mistakes. Never let those mistakes achieve a higher importance than you deserve. Sooner or later all human beings will make a mistake, but that needn't define you forever. It is a point in time when you elected to take one action instead of another. That is all it is and it can happen to anyone. It does not have to be the dominant thought of the day. People do forgive and forget and life will move on.

If your conversation is full of "I should" do this, that or the other thing, you are also exhibiting danger signs of low self-esteem. It means you are thinking about doing, but not doing. The same goes for the "I must" school of thought. Maybe you should and maybe you shouldn't. You don't need to block yourself in with such imperative thoughts.

To boost your self-esteem, nothing is more important than staying positive and reminding yourself of all the parts of your life that are good. Keeping a gratitude journal where you take a few minutes each day to make notes of all the things you have to be thankful for is an excellent way to remind yourself of what is working well in your life.

At least once a week, list your accomplishments. Think about all that was involved in achieving those things, the effort and the skill and the thought that went into what you did, and give yourself a mental pat on the back. Clearly you are capable of blending many components of yourself to an excellent result.

If a thought keeps returning to your mind, marring your concentration and bringing down your mood, it may seem too big a step to get it out of your head. If you cannot banish it, at least frame it differently. When you feel your thoughts going negative think about how you could look at the situation differently. Can you turn the negative into a positive? What parts of the situation look brighter if viewed from a different perspective?

When you achieve small successes, rejoice in them and feel positive. Allow yourself to feel success by breaking big projects down into smaller more measurable tasks.

If your self-esteem is normally strong and healthy, but certain situations cause it to tumble, take a long, hard look at the circumstances that impact your mood. Are they linked to a specific person, to a particular work or recreational situation? Sometimes something as a television show can throw off your mood because one of the characters triggers a dark childhood memory.

When you know what it is that tumbles your self-esteem from healthy to shaky, you will be better able to avoid it or reframe it.

Another self-esteem savior can be stepping away from yourself, including your innermost negative thoughts, and looking at them from a different perspective. You might write about them rapidly as they cross your mind and record everything in your journal. Some therapists suggest that if you are right handed, you try to write out disturbing thoughts with your left hand, and vice versa, giving your brain a specific cue that you need a different perspective on this thought.

It can also be therapeutic to turn your nagging thoughts into a poem or into a song. Sometimes the very act of creating something around a bad experience can be quite cathartic.

Many researchers support the idea of practicing mindfulness as a way of understanding your thoughts are just ideas flitting through your mind, and you don't have to let them control the moment you are in.

In this case, you can be aware that certain thoughts are troubling you, but your mind also signals that you have had a good meal, the sun is shining on you, the warm breeze cools your skin and there are fragrant flowers in the meadow across the road. Give yourself into what is fine about this moment and instead of doing battle to remove certain thoughts, you instead incorporate the beautiful moments into the present.

Chapter 12: The broader scope of narcissism

Narcissism has existed for hundreds of years as a human personality disorder, but it was only in 2008 when the full concept of what narcissism can really do to a life made headlines.

At that time, one-time potential United States presidential candidate John Edwards used his own self-acknowledged narcissism as an excuse for his extramarital affair with Reille Hunter, a videographer.

In an interview with Bob Woodruff on the ABC News show *Nightline*, Edwards acknowledge the affair and made it clear his wife and his God had forgiven him.

His responses to Woodruff's questions were masterful. He was at times contrite, at times aggressive and defensive, and never ready to admit that he had just screwed up.

Edwards blamed everything not on himself, but on his narcissism. He admitted to his complete self-focus and egotism as part of his overall condition of believing he could do anything he desired and not be responsible for it.

While many dismissed his claim at the time or suggested he was using a possible medical condition to justify what he had done, we know from previous chapters that perhaps Edwards was actually stating the truth.

He showed many of the conditions of narcissism, including practicing extreme behavior, lying and refusing to repent and report that he had learned anything from his mistake.

His description of his narcissistic condition also caused the spotlight to move closer to the center of narcissism and to focus the public eye on it. Could narcissism be the reason so many talented and famous people seem unable to lead normal lifestyles?

The late cultural historian Christopher Lasch had been predicting that since the late 1970s. His book *The Culture of Narcissism: American Life in an Age of Diminishing Expectations,* centered on the theme that narcissism would become more prevalent in the years to come because of our society's fostering of it culturally, psychologically, artistically and historically.

North American society, post Second World War, had changed the family structure to produce children with personalities that could technically be described as pathological narcissism. He looked at the utopia of the 1960s, followed by the era of "personal growth" in the 1970s, and linked it together to form the basis for a world that focused increasingly on the individual and their dreams and less on the concept of submission to a common good.

Lasch's book is particularly insightful on the subject because although it is full of fascinating facts and examples, it is done generally in a non-judgmental style. He doesn't write to suggest one era or one style of personal growth is better than another; rather he approaches his subject with an open curiosity. His observations are clinical in nature, not malicious. He is employing a cultural change and its impact.

By the time our social history had moved on to the John Edwards affair and his references to narcissism, it was clear that many modern politicians were exhibiting classic signs of narcissism. They were not interested in playing by the rules; they had grandiose ideas and a sense of entitlement.

People at all levels of life and work started to believe, perhaps for the first time in our history, that they "deserved" to have a good life and they were going to take it.

The "Me" Generation arrived, determined to achieve personal happiness first, and consider other people second.

As each generation gains its stake in our culture, their sense of self-worth grew stronger until in 2010, two psychology professors actually labeled the trend *The Narcissism Epidemic* in their book with the same title.

The professors, W. Keith Campbell and Jean Twenge, describe a rapidly rising rate of Americans who have been diagnosed with a Narcissistic Personality Disorder.

In the book, they identified a number of narcissistic trends that can have a serious impact on our culture as we know it.

For example, narcissists are less likely to build long-term stable relationships with a single partner with whom they raise a family. Instead, they do not want to make such an investment of their energy and emotion. They seek short-term, shallower relationships that preclude any serious commitment.

Narcissists also believe the entire world is watching them and they love it. They want even more attention. The authors report one case of a narcissist who hired fake paparazzi to run after them for a weekend, just to show other people how important they were.

Young narcissists took to social media like Facebook, My Space and Twitter to broadcast to the world everything from what they had or didn't have for breakfast, how many beers they drank with friends, their most mundane thoughts and banal activities. They fed their grandiose sense of self with even the most basic details, convinced that the world at large hung on every action and observation they made.

In fact, it was by watching how profiles were changing on My Space that prompted the authors' study of narcissism.

They saw how what was originally just healthy self-esteem was evolving into narcissism.

So concerned were they that they concluded it was time for the nation to come together and try to change young people's attitudes by emphasizing social skills like sharing and empathy and by practicing thankfulness.

They expressed concern for a generation which grew up feeling entitled to excellent jobs with mentoring bosses and had a lot of trouble coping when reality hit them between the eyes. Their inability to compromise led to anger and then despair.

"As long as you're happy," became the reassurance from adoring parents and supportive friends.

Even programs of therapy built to combat addictive habits like drinking and gambling are totally built around the "me" theme. "I am an alcoholic," says the person seeking help, and from there forward, it is all about their thoughts and needs and plans as they work their way to sobriety.

As a result, today's self-aware and self-indulgent youth are more apt to progress to full blown

Narcissistic Personality Disorder than generations that preceded them.

Commenting on the book, Dr. Robert L. Leahy, author of *Anxiety Free: Unravel Your Fears Before They Unravel You,* said it is obvious now that narcissism is on the rise and it is time re-rescue our culture from ourselves.

There is no denying that many parents today see their job as one of shoveling on constant praise, trading gifts for good behavior, and relentlessly assuring little ones that they are pretty, gifted and special. Still hurting from a harsher existence when they were young, they vow that their children will go into this world with a strong sense of self-worth and assurance that they can be anything they want to be.

We look up to people whose egos show no sign of modesty, whether it is a socialite like Paris Hilton or an entrepreneur like Donald Trump whose name is boldly emblazoned on all that he owns.

Social media means anyone can be a star, even without going through the formal protocols of the past. Authors can have bestsellers they publish themselves, musicians can produce their music independently and win millions of followers, and people with unique ideas can create one YouTube video and become a sensational hit within just a few days.

The National Institutes of Health has released figures showing that Narcissistic Personality Disorder for people in their 20s is three times more likely to occur than to people 65 or older.

Is the future that grim for our upcoming generation?

Not really. Just as this trend towards narcissism has grown in recent years, so too will it likely recede as the millenials grow up and have children of their own. Having someone you love more than yourself can weaken your tendency towards narcissism.

Plus, the millenials are showing great ability to deal with technological change and to be upbeat and optimistic about new developments in the future. They are quick to take advantages of new technology and to adapt it to their lifestyle, important skills for survival in the future.

Perhaps in their own way they will be a positive force for change in the workplace. If they are unwilling to put up with sexism, racism, and bullying, their impact could be significant and a force for good.

But a society too close to the edge of narcissism would be a dangerous and dark place to live. Each person would live their life like a contestant on Survivor, confident that the end justifies the means and where manipulation of others and lack of empathy for them is a sign of strength.

If people took all the things they felt entitled too, crime would also be on the rise. Everyone would believe themselves beautiful and be on a quest to become even more striking, so sales of cosmetics and plastic surgery would skyrocket.

Relationships would be shallow and home life could be dismal. The world of narcissism gone wild would be a sad and lonely society.

Not every psychologist believes that is where we are headed. In a survey called "Monitoring the Future," published in *Perspectives on Psychological Science,* researchers Trzesniewski and Donnellan concluded that while there was a hike in materialism, it did not translated to a complete change in attitudes and behavior in youth.

In fact, as they reported, each generation has its army of selfless volunteers and its narcissists. History has shown that repeatedly, and the generation just growing into adulthood now will be no different.

Others also rise to the defense of social media, saying it really has little to do with fueling narcissism. People who want to boast about themselves have always found a way. People were worried that the telephone was a tool for mindless self-promotion when it first came out.

Many young people using social media sites use them to promote a world where bullying is ended, where poverty is tackled and where the environment is protected. Many send endless, harmless messages that help them develop lasting, deeper friendships that will be a support system for life.

Others post blogs and Tweets to affirm their principles and to practice the growth and development of themselves. They explore ideas and invite comments and discussion on topics of interest in their world.

If you are a parent and want to help your child develop a self-esteem but stay far from the edges of serious narcissism, what should you focus your efforts on?

Empathy is a good place to start. Once your children are aware of the feelings of other people and learn to consider the impact of their actions on others, they will rarely become narcissistic.

In fact, many social scientists believe that of all the living skills parents can teach their children, the fostering of empathy is crucial. By this we mean teaching a child to be sensitive to the feelings of other people. Without it, it is virtually impossible to sustain a healthy relationship in life.

For example, in *The Big Bang Theory*, the popular television show, Sheldon is so self-centered that it is difficult for him to have friends. His personality borders on narcissism.

Nobody can sit in his place on the sofa. He draws up the terms to all his relationships in complicated agreements.

But through the quiet coaching of those who live with him, Sheldon has learned that there are circumstances when he must think of other people. He has learned that making someone a hot cup of tea when they are stressed is the acceptable response to their grief or anxiety. While he is not a naturally kind and thoughtful person, his narcissism has not progressed to the point where he can't even consider that not everyone feels as he does about things in life.

Children learn empathy by observing it in their caregivers and the people around them. They watch people's body language and listen to changing tones of voices. They observe far more than most adults realize, and what they see forms the foundation of how they treat others in their lives.

If they witness respect and consideration for others, they will practice respect and consideration as they grow up. If they see contempt and mockery and are reminded constantly by their parents that "looking after number one" is what matters, that is what they will value as they grow.

One of the most effective ways to teach your children empathy is to practice it on them. When they are frustrated, instead of dictating to them the way they should feel or behave, the parent can instead practice empathy by acknowledging that the child is upset.

The parent says something like "I can see you are upset about this. You are frustrated because you can't get your doll into those clothes aren't you? Is that something I can help you with?"

Parents can also teach empathy by taking the time to explain to children why others are around them are feeling sad or happy. This teaches the child to be aware that other people have feelings too and that they are triggered by a series of events that happen within their own lives.

For example, a parent can say "Grammy is feeling sad today because one of her best friends died. If she comes by later, be sure to be especially kind to her today and give her a really good hug."

Or they might say, "Your friend Laura's father just found out he is sick. She may be upset tomorrow; be sure you are a special friend and support her. She needs a little extra kindness right now."

You can remind children about empathy when you observe it in cartoon characters and people in television shows as well. Watching a scary movie, as the heroine goes to investigate a noise in the basement, you might remark: "she must be really scared to go down there."

When reading your children bedtime stories, invite them to discuss how they think the person in the book feels when they have to deal with some drama. It can start with something simple like: "Do you think Rapunzel is sad because she is locked in the tower?"

All of these things subtly remind children that other people have feelings and they should be sensitive to them.

You can teach children about empathy, but you have to be careful not to preach to them about it. Little children who are upset about something, or are angry or sad will not be in any mood to think about anyone but themselves. If you push too hard, they will push you away, unable to deal with it at the moment.

It is best to wait until calm has been restored before resuming your "lessons."

We may be able to help prevent children from turning into narcissists through subtly engaging them in practices of empathy, and we may be able to teach ourselves to recognize narcissists, but what we cannot do is actually change the narcissist.

Our time is better invested in teaching ourselves how to deal with them and keep them from assuming control of our lives or torpedoing our careers.

For example, when the narcissist is raging, you can walk away saying calmly that you need a cup of tea and return after he or she has had a few minutes to calm down.

When you want to get your point across to a narcissist, always remember the "I not you" rule. Say "I want to discuss my position on this subject" instead of "you should listen to my position on this subject."

You can share your point of view, and to check to see if any part of it has registered with the narcissist, you can ask, "Of my point of view, is there any aspect that you believe has merit?"

Try to keep the atmosphere calm and level when dealing with a narcissist. When they are angry, they are much more difficult.

Finally, if we are to ensure that our world really does not sustain an epidemic of narcissism, how can you help yourself if you are noticing that you are increasingly preoccupied with your life and your world?

First, take time out to seriously take stock of yourself. Of the habits you know you have that border on narcissism, are some getting worse? Do you find yourself increasingly intolerant of the apparent stupidity of others? Do you find that you are becoming chronically late because it is obvious to you that what you are doing is clearly more important than the things people are putting off waiting for you? Do you enjoy that sense of power?

If you recognize even one habit that borders on narcissism that seems to be getting worse, try to change it next week. Make a real effort to show up on time for once, or to acknowledge that even one other person that you know or have read about has something special intellectually to contribute to this world of ours.

Make a real effort to listen with empathy to at least one person a day. Like Sheldon, think about one appropriate behavior you can summon when a person turns to you in their time of distress.

Practice empathy by attempting to explain something that you do or feel strongly about to another person. Discuss the details of what you want them to understand, and then learn to step back politely and ask something like "Does any of this make sense to you?" It shows that at least you are considering the other person.

If you are spending an increasing amount of time fantasizing about greatness for yourself, take time out to consider what really is special about yourself, whether you are on stage or in company with other people. Try to build your own self-esteem with an honest assessment of your success or talent. It is okay to tell yourself every once in a while that you did a great job.

Mentally close the shades on the prying eyes you feel are always watching you. Go for a walk in nature where you will not run into people who you believe are judging you. Even if you feel shameful about something you do, try to relax and realize that people's attention spans are so preoccupied with other things that your slip from the imaginary pedestal would likely not even have been noticed.

Above all, keep in mind that even if you are perilously close to stepping off the edge of self-esteem and into the deep, dark world of narcissism, that you can still pull yourself back. You are intelligent, you are driven, and you are capable of tackling any challenge. Make your next challenge one to build a healthy sense of self so you won't have to resort to bragging and making extraordinary claims about yourself. People will love you as you are; you just have to give them a chance.

Conclusion

If you are living with a narcissist and unable to let go of their hold on your life, you must find the strength to establish your boundaries and if that doesn't work, to leave.

Acceptance of what a narcissist is and how they behave is the key to any life with such a person in it. You may actually be able to make marriage with a narcissist work, for example, if you are able to maintain your own strength and independence and yet provide them with a situation they find beneficial to themselves.

At the same time, you cannot innocently assume that if you just try to do things a little better that they will be pleased and they will appreciate your efforts. Life with a narcissist doesn't work that way.

You will be more apt to find the courage you need to get out of your life with the narcissist if you understand why you were attracted to them in the first place and why you are still holding off packing when you likely should have left years ago.

You may have become so beat up mentally, emotionally and perhaps even physically to have any confidence left to believe that you deserve better in life. You may have developed an addiction to your narcissistic partner and you want to go but you believe you just can't live without them.

Perhaps you remember the happy days of your first attraction to the narcissist in your life. You recall their charm and how easily they talked of love and marriage, even in an age where lots of other people seemed afraid of commitment. Those were heady, fun-filled days and they stay strong in your memory, and you yearn and dream that someday they will come back.

That dream is a drug and you have to break your addiction. Those bright, happy days are history now and what is before you is the darkness and continuing growth of the narcissistic personality.

When it becomes increasingly apparent that the drug of those happy days with your charming partner are gone forever, you can go into a kind of withdrawal syndrome. Your drug of choice is no longer available to you. Like any other addict, you are disoriented and dazed and weakened with your addiction that is not being fed.

You don't understand what happened that the love drug isn't yours to take anymore. You wonder if you did something to kill it, and that makes you even more depressed.

Even when you realize that there is no more of the drug you crave available to you, one day your partner shows you the smallest kindness, or what you interpret to be a kindness, and you are back like an addict to your old habits and your old dreams.

Like any other addict who finally breaks the horrible cycle of dependency, you must leave your narcissist and refuse to ever indulge in that dream that everything will be loving and okay again.

You must mentally as well as physically leave a narcissist. Not only must you try to have no contact with them in person, you must try to remove them from your thoughts. This is what psychotherapists label a toxic relationship. It is a road to nowhere and will lead to darkness and hurt for you.

While scientific studies are indicating that narcissistic behavior seems to be becoming more prevalent in our society, we must still be cognizant that Narcissistic Personality Disorder is relatively rare.

As experts at The Mayo Clinic point out, almost all children and teenagers show signs of narcissism, but a lot of that behavior is typical of their age and it will change as they mature and find their place in the world.

More men than women fall prey to full-blown Narcissistic Personality Disorder, but science is unable to tell us why. In such cases, it usually begins when they are in their teens or early twenties.

At this point of this book, you will have determined whether or not you are a narcissist. If you are, we urge you to seek professional therapy to allow yourself the opportunity to reconstruct your life and live it more fully.

To be a narcissist is, in essence, to be deprived of many of the things that make us human: our ability to really learn to know ourselves, our joy in learning to truly love and appreciate others, and to open up our heart and talents to do meaningful work.

Psychotherapy can help you create deeper relationships and relate better to others in a world built on a foundation of strong relationships. It will help you understand why you behave as you do and overcome your contempt for others, and more importantly, your deep dislike of yourself in your darker stages.

You will receive help in maintaining relationships with your work colleagues and with your neighbors in your community.

Gradually, over time, you will come to see a more realistic picture of who you are and the genuine skills and talents that you have. You will move from your fantasy world to the real world and find that it is not just bearable, but better than that.

You will learn how to set more realistic goals for yourself and take pleasure within yourself for your accomplishments instead of depending on others to feed your ego.

There is no denying that undergoing therapy for narcissism is difficult. By the very nature of your condition, you will feel it is not necessary and that you are achieving nothing from it. You will want to quit.

You must summon everything within you and stick to it. Note the small changes that occur over time. Attend all of your scheduled sessions and do homework and take any medications as directed.

If you have accompanying issues of drug or alcohol abuse or mental health problems, a situation that is not uncommon, be sure to secure treatment for them as well.

You owe it not just to the other people in your life, but to yourself.

You may think that you love yourself now, but in reality, you can only really begin a satisfying relationship with yourself after therapy when you can get to know the real you.

If you have recognized through this book that you are living with a narcissist, you may also need professional guidance to help you accept and deal with the situation, whether it means trying to work at improving the relationship or ending it.

It is important that you find ways to deal with the narcissist in your life while still protecting yourself and your own need for a life rich with fulfillment and solid relationships.

If the narcissist in your life is a child, seek help as soon as possible to try to alter the child's behavior and help them build empathy. If it is a sibling or a spouse, express your willingness to participate in therapy sessions and realize that while you may not be able to change the narcissist's behavior, you can control the impact it has on you.

Most importantly, understand that it is impossible to feed the fire of the narcissistic ego. You will never have enough admiration and assurance and the more you stoke the fire, the more fuel it will need.

You will also be subjected to anger and different forms of abuse and any weakness you show will be used against you. Being vulnerable is a luxury you cannot afford if you live with a narcissist.

Take time to take care of yourself in the midst of the chaos around you. Try to make yoga or meditation or similar practices part of your day to retain your own center of calm and tranquility.

Most of all, know that your life and your goals have value and nobody has the right to take that away from you. As ill as they may be with narcissism, find a way to continue to live your life to the fullest.

Other books available by author on Kindle, paperback and audio

Emotionally Abusive and Verbally Abusive Relationships: Causes and Effects, Analysis and Solutions